Funeral Playlist

Funeral Playlist Songs

Also by Sarah Gorham

Alpine Apprentice (University of Georgia Press)

Study in Perfect (University of Georgia Press)

Bad Daughter (Four Way Books)

The Cure (Four Way Books)

The Tension Zone (Four Way Books)

Don't Go Back to Sleep (Galileo Press)

Last Call: Poems on Alcoholism, Addiction, and Deliverance
(Anthology, edited by Sarah Gorham and Jeffrey Skinner, Sarabande Books, Inc.)

On *Alpine Apprentice*

A palpable, loving evocation of experiences "tucked deep" into the author's soul.
— *Kirkus Reviews*

In tones stunningly crisp, rapturous, and sure, Sarah Gorham has taken the book-length essay to a place of high art.
— Mary Cappello, *Life Breaks In: A Mood Almanack*

Sarah Gorham's *Alpine Apprentice...* is animated by curiosity more than self-centeredness, and the author's decision to broaden the thematic and associative range of materials is entirely well founded. It is a book of great sensibility.
— Tony Hoagland

On *Study in Perfect*

Easily one of the best books I read this year was Sarah Gorham's gorgeous, one-of-a-kind *Study in Perfect*.
— Katy Waldman, *Slate*

This superb collection from Gorham... exemplifies the best in creative nonfiction...
— *Publishers Weekly*, starred review

It's not often that I encounter a writer whose prose is this precise and lyrical and whose imaginative leaps are as articulate, unpredictable, and entertaining.
— *Bernard Cooper*

Funeral Playlist

by Sarah Gorham

Etruscan Press

Etruscan Press
Wilkes University
84 West South Street
Wilkes-Barre, PA 18766
(570) 408-4546

Wilkes
University

www.etruscanpress.org

Published 2024 by Etruscan Press
Printed in the United States of America
Cover art: ©RMN-Grand Palais/Art Resource, NY.
Cover design by Logan Rock
Interior design and typesetting by Joseph Schwartz
The text of this book is set in Garamond.

First Edition

17 18 19 20 5 4 3 2 1

Library of Congress Cataloging-in-Publication Data

Names: Gorham, Sarah, 1954- author.
Title: Funeral Playlist | by Sarah Gorham
Description: First edition. | Wilkes-Barre, PA : Etruscan Press, 2024.
Summary: "Using her own "funeral playlist," Sarah Gorham examines the intricate connections between music, consolation, and human mortality"-- Provided by publisher.
Identifiers: LCCN 2023038963 | ISBN 9798988198512 (trade paperback)
          ISBN 9798988198529 (ebook)
Subjects: LCGFT: Essays.
Classification: LCC PS3557.O7554 F86 2024 | DDC 814/.54--dc23/eng/20231113
LC record available at https://lccn.loc.gov/2023038963

Please turn to the back of this book for a list of the sustaining funders of Etruscan Press.

This book is printed on recycled, acid-free paper.

"When I'm writing a sentence,
I automatically sound it out in my head."

— Haruki Murakami, *Absolutely on Music: Conversations*

"If a passage occurs twice,
it is played slower the second time;
if three times, still slower."

— Wolfgang Amadeus Mozart

"At some point the gong sounds, calling them all to supper.
Then her granddaughter comes back up from sunbathing on the
dock, humming quietly to herself, just as she has done all her life,
even as a little girl. Which means that in the end there are certain
things you can take with you when you flee, things that have no
weight, such as music."

— Jenny Erpenbeck, *Visitation*

For Jeffrey

Funeral Playlist

Author's Note

I've long kept a folder on my laptop containing melancholy music. A rather gloomy practice, I'll admit. But my focus tilts naturally toward the dark side, where questions and challenges are (for me) substantial and worth pursuing. One day it occurred to me that this file could be seen as a playlist for my own funeral, an idea with all the necessary components for a consequential and various project. Why not use it to examine how music and mortality connect?

Just as there are varieties of music, there are many kinds of death within each human: the quick passage of childhood, the narrowing of parenting as a daughter or son heads off to college, the going away of animals we love, a serious diagnosis, estrangement, the early death of a parent, and the slow but sure signs of one's own aging. No life in its many stages is without bereavement. And, whether it's the thunder and brilliance of Mozart's *Requiem*, the sultry, somber notes of Nina Simone's love song, or the simple Irish melody of "The Parting Glass," elegiac music gives us access to deeper regions of thought and imagination.

In these essays I ask the question "What is the sound of mourning?" In "Perchoo," for example, I use the doleful call of the mourning dove as a touchstone. In another, a mother sits alongside her premature baby in the NICU, playing and replaying "King and Lionheart" as if it were a lullaby for the child (and her). "Be Dark Night," a dirge-like indie song, summons both beautiful and frightening images. The essay "*Amarilli mia bella*" dramatizes the link between love and death, and an amateur's efforts to sing the seventeenth century aria in her voice lessons.

I have interviewed a conductor, a classical pianist, professors, a woman with synesthesia, teachers of music, and an indie songwriter. Such experiences have informed my work, allowing me to move a little closer to an acceptance of my own mortality. Death, of course, is the ultimate uncertainty and what happens afterward—heaven or nothingness or something in between—is the greatest unknown. While writing these essays, the one thing that became clear to me, is our need for music to feel less alone, from our beginnings to our end. We crave connection, and there is no more direct route between us than music. As Whitman wrote, "We were together. I forget the rest."

"Perchoo," or the Music of Mourning

Song

It's below freezing, and the maple, cherry, sycamore, and beech trees are stripped to their bones. Most animals are silent, sleeping away their territoriality and sexual insistence, or wintering in milder climes. The mourning dove sits on a knotty branch, its silhouette black, as the sun dissolves into the grass. What is the sound of mourning? Consider the dove, its plaintive call—*Perchoo-oo-oo-o*—sound slurring up and fading into a kind of musical ellipses. What elegant pining. What perfect music for the transition from evening into night, fear into lament. After death there should be a bird, and why not the mourning dove? We imagine the bird speaks to us—*Ah-YOU-you-you-you*. How human it is to transpose, to carry what is wordless into our own field of aural signs, our language.

Four sisters, each of them, shy of adulthood, sit on the floor outside their mother's bedroom. There she lies dying, there she has asked for a little solitude. Maybe she needs to pull her thoughts together, or wants to sleep, or wishes for a break from the guilt of "putting them through this." Outside her door, seated cross-legged on the wall-to-wall carpet, they carry on their chorus of sniffles and sneezes, stutters, and coughs. The air conditioner churns away. The balled-up tissues pile up. They are angry or lost or just plain devastated. This was supposed to be a cancer easily cured. A few snips of the scalpel. And here, six months from diagnosis, their mother is lying on her bed, pale and skeletal at fifty-one.

The sisters need solace, and the mother has always been the primary source of solace. But she can no longer deliver it.

Outside, the heat settles like a double wall around the house. Cicadas thrum and fall in layers under tree branches. A Good Humor truck jingles by and here comes the neighbor, strolling across the street to deliver what he most surely thought was a considerate, caring query. So great to see the sun today, right? *How's your mother doing?*

Why answer the doorbell? Why, the very next day, open the door to the delivery boy who holds out our dry cleaning hooked on his index finger, then launches into an enthusiastic sales pitch—a "subscription" to his service—minutes after our mother takes her last rusty breath?

I try to imitate the dove cooing from its perch, but my lips quiver like a leaf edge, then cramp.

The mourning dove *(Zinaida macroura)* is the state bird of Wisconsin, birthplace of my mother and many of her relatives. Her brother and his wife lost their son to a terrible accident. First came the inquiries: was the driver on drugs? Who sold him the drugs? Were they being chased? Was the car itself at fault—slippage in the brakes, a faulty seatbelt? Later they lapsed into silence, keeping up the appearance of dignified calm—silence over the breakfast table, slow motion reaching for the cream and the coffee and the blackberry scones. Newspaper pages turned one after the other, without being seen, then—that full stare into the beyond. Finished with their doubts and arguments, they buried their sorrow, and were careful not to listen to certain music, especially the songs their teenager loved. We sisters were not taken by surprise by my mother's death as they were. We had six months to say goodbye. But not enough, never enough.

There are countless ways to mourn, as many as there are individuals. There are those who cannot touch their feelings. "And they, since they/Were not the one dead, turned to their affairs," wrote Robert Frost. Others say they need time to complete their grieving, or simply want to put it on a shelf for later. If you don't sing, or cry, or talk about death, it may not exist. On the other end of the spectrum, the Irish have their keening as the deceased is removed from the house—*your mother will miss you, your daughter will miss you, your sister will miss you, your niece will miss you.* Puebloans in the desert believe the cry of a mourning dove will draw them to water, to the springs and pools where the birds come to drink, especially at twilight. They call them rain doves and the dove feathers are tied to prayer sticks so that the people can use them as invocations to water itself. Towards the end of her life, my mother refused to eat or drink, even water. She wrote a note to each of us to make sure we knew she loved us: *I have a terrible thirst for you girls.* We sisters took turns laying our bodies over her body kissing her cool forehead and cheeks and hands.

Sobbing swells up your face and reddens your eyes and makes your nose run profusely. Sobbing follows the rate of respiration, indeed amplifies it—an ancient phone ringing from a time before its invention. But tears themselves make no music. They pool inside the lower eyelid, trickle soundlessly down the face. If we feel like crying, it may be possible for adults to distract ourselves, stop those tears before they start. But once begun, arresting their flow is far more difficult. For the most part, children do not have either option. As we are well aware, they cry more than grown-ups. Sometimes the family is so broken, they can't even attend the funeral.

Cross culturally, humans make sounds in response to the loss of a loved one. Though the rites vary from place to place, we seem eager to fill the void with something that distracts, erasing the silence that so persistently reminds us of the voice we no longer hear. Even animals mourn. Most famous are the elephants that congregate about the body in something like a wake, sniffing and caressing. They even return later, repeatedly, to visit the skeletons, lifting their trunks to their mouths to taste what they are smelling. And birds exhibit the semblance of grief. Their brains, after all, are wired with nerve connections and hormones similar to ours. Mourning doves will watch over their deceased, stroke them with their bills, and later return to the place where they died. But this behavior must go on for a long time to prove it's some kind of grief. It might be mere confusion, and unless we could simultaneously observe the bird's hippocampus light up on a scan, we can't be sure. After all, birds don't imagine the future or suffer from a tragedy in the past. They don't plan or regret, cannot understand a lifespan, or anticipate their own death. They sing to attract a mate or signal danger, the most basic of communication. Humans have language and music to soothe a dying mother. I remember the Schumann that drifted from her room. The Traümerei were her favorite. Schumann singing from centuries ago—the feathery touch of the pianist, the repeated passages that flitted and rippled through the hall. My mother loved Schumann, though I'm not sure what it said to her in her dying. To me it said, *you'll be safe, someday the sorrow will dissolve into the future. And when it's over and your mother is gone, Schumann—and the dove—will bring her back.*

Diet

Mourning doves will consume a huge variety of seeds, more so than any other North American bird. They particularly like sunflower, safflower, white millet, and chopped corn, but these are often quickly scarfed up by squirrels, and other birds higher in the pecking order. The cheap bags of seed almost always contain loads of red millet. It's filler, and only when the squirrels and the more aggressive birds finish their meal do the doves arrive on the scene with their flexible appetites. There's more variety if they eat in the wild with its wheat, corn, canary grass, and pokeberry seeds. But it's dangerous because predators are comfortable there too.

I remember my mother splitting a roasted chicken into seven parts, reserving just the back and maybe one wing for herself. She also used the heels of Pepperidge Farm bread for her own sandwiches. She claimed they were her favorites. I'm sure this was a lie, or something she just convinced herself of over the years. Where hunger was concerned, her family came first. After she died, all sorts of food arrived at our doorstep—baked hams, macaroni casseroles with Durkee onions, biscuits, fruit breads, and baskets of fried chicken—all with a simple "Sorry for your loss," or just plain "Sorry." If there had been Edible Arrangements back then, they too would have piled up on our dining room table or stuffed into the basement fridge.

My mother lunched the way her mother had lunched—discretely, standing in the kitchen, holding a small white saucer with sliced sweet pickles, cheese, and a Baby Ruth bar for dessert. While I grieved, I threw my health to the wind eating only sketchy foods like canned enchiladas or roast beef hash, fried chicken livers with eggs, brie cheese, and Lays potato chips. I wrote a message in the fog on my window: Help me. Backwards, so it could be seen from the street.

In the independent film *A Ghost Story*, Rooney Mara plays a woman called "M" who has lost her husband to a car accident that occurred on the street, right outside their home. A friend shows up with a cherry pie. She leaves and soon after, "M" grabs the pie and a fork and slinks down to the kitchen floor. She proceeds to eat, slowly at first, then accelerating her pace, forkful after forkful, stuffing her mouth, wolfing it down, barely pausing to swallow until she has consumed the entire pie. It is one of the most riveting, effective depictions of grief I've ever seen.

Grief makes the world seem foreign, flat, and strange. Grieving, we watch from a distance as people fuss and fume about trivial things. The heel of one woman's shoe breaks off on a New York sidewalk and she swears like a sailor. A man leans on his horn, raging as another car cuts him off. What is the point of this caterwauling over dropped keys, parking places, a butter knife fallen to the floor? What are these things compared to the enormity of a death? As for all those well-intentioned attempts at sympathy, they don't really make a dent: You know, my uncle died too, when I was just seventeen. The subtext is so obvious: My grief was at least as intense as yours. You'll get over it.

Not helpful, we think, and retreat deeper inside, free of their noise. We feel only what we feel, our ears plugged, and vision clouded. Indeed, it's typical for mourners to think only of themselves, a condition some call the "zoom lens effect." Easier to scarf up a pie, or focus on those small slices of pickle, crackers, and cheese—arranging a meal so the best smidgen comes last, then pressing our index finger into each crumb and drawing it to our mouth. Ah-ME-me-me-me. Not Ah-YOU-you-you-you. Anything else feels naked and dangerous.

Range

Mourning doves are tolerant of human settlements and thus have quite an extraordinary range, stretching from parts of Canada, throughout the States, and across both Mexico and the Caribbean. Some estimate their numbers to be close to 120 million. Unfortunately, they're a favorite of hunters who kill close to twenty million annually. Then, consider the fact that they are ground feeders, prey not just for sportsmen, but cats and hawks and other predators. Finally, for some odd reason a dove will freeze motionless till its song is complete, even in the chase. For many reasons, this sotto voce singer is an easy target.

Once I was a teenage killer of mourning doves. As part of a seventh-grade curriculum in the natural sciences, I took turns working on a bird-banding team consisting of three other teenagers supervised by a respected ornithologist, botanist, and middle school teacher. Our classroom was stocked with Roger Tory Peterson guides and Zim's *Birds of North America*, the walls hung with identification points, distribution charts, and more. We built birdhouses and feeders filled with suet we made ourselves from bacon grease and seed. We wrote bird life histories, traipsed lightly through the woods with binoculars and scopes, and competed fiercely for the longest life list.

A thicket stood outside our building with a mostly protected grassy area in front—the perfect setting for capturing birds. We hung mist nets between the trees and set out five or six cages in the clearing. I specifically remember one such structure—with nine compartments, three across and three down, like a tic-tac-toe board—each with a swirl of multi-color seeds leading up and a trick platform a bird need only rest one foot on, causing the door to slide down. It was intended for the smallest ground feeders (sparrows, wrens, chickadees, titmice). Occasionally, larger birds showed up too.

We followed a strict code of ethics. First: do no harm. The team leader checked traps and nets repeatedly, then shut, or took them down in the evening and when predators were present. Seed was stored in a large, plastic-lined garbage can and we used a sawed-off bleach bottle as a scooper. Once a white-throated, house, or song sparrow was trapped, we held it with utmost care, its head between middle and index finger, its body cupped in our palm, secured by a pinky and thumb. If we worked gently and quietly, and completed the process quickly, the bird would be minimally traumatized. There were specialized tools for affixing the band and ensuring no painful overlap. These were arranged in boxes by size: miniature, medium, and large, with a couple of extra larges in case we happened to net a Pileated or crow. We recorded data in a binder, adding it to wall-sized charts and graphs, noting species, dates, and the numbers stamped on the bird bracelets.

I was a nervous team leader—so determined to do no harm, I tried to scare the birds away by banging on the window or stomping on the walkway that surrounded our classroom. They scattered quickly. Better no banding at all than an unmanageable cluster of snared and terrified prisoners. Inevitably, the birds returned, and I was not watching when the dove, a female, waddled forward, head down into the tiniest compartment, its weight bringing the door down almost instantly. Nor was I present while it hurled itself against the mesh, tearing tissue and slicing open a skin just above the eye. Blood began to soak into its feathers and, finally spotting this calamity, I ran for help. Our teacher was irritated at the interruption, then furious. He wrapped his hands around the bird, dabbed a bit of ointment on the wounds and then, abandoning protocol, released it to its foreshortened life. Indeed, the dove didn't make it far at all and stood panting at thicket's edge. The image of this iridescent creature with its mangled feathers and flesh was wrenching. It was the first black mark on my conscience and introduced my earliest experience of grief, one layered with guilt and the horror of killing something, especially this gentle bird. Not surprising that I remember it in such detail.

The word "bereave" comes from the Old English bereafian meaning "to be snatched violently away" or "robbed of," and most tellingly, "to be torn apart."

Flight

A human opens fire in the woods, a door slams, or there's a cat circling. Birds immediately startle, flushing at the speed of alarm. And this is what it sounds like when doves cry: a fluttering whistle, especially on take-off. While other birds generate only the thud of wings, the dove creates an extra layer of music called "sonation," from the Latin sonare "to sound." A sonata, for example, is music played, rather than sung. The dove's whinny is produced by air vibrating against the contoured tips of its flight feathers. It too has a purpose, a presaging of danger, like the white underside of a deer's tail or a sudden branch snapping in a forest.

After our mother died, my sisters and I scattered into four different cities, four different states, where we mourned in four different ways. There was no gathering around the kitchen table, no sharing of music or poetry that might comfort, no laughter-inducing stories of that terrible vacation or heart-to-heart conversations while our mother cleaned up in the kitchen, no sifting through clothes and letters and purses. There was no discussion at all; we just went on with our lives. We were used to pouring out our troubles with her, and no one else.

I taught English at a private high school in New York surrounded by hormonally charged adolescents and a handful of other teachers who hadn't yet faced the pre-mature death of a loved one. I felt like the single citizen on an undiscovered planet, climbing the stairs to my sad little apartment, over-preparing my lessons for the next day, and later, rewarding myself with brainless stuff like *Family Feud* or *National Enquirer* while the trees went black against a lavender-smudged sky. I don't recall the landscape at all and certainly no birds, though a mourning dove with its ancient music would have been pleasant, another voice mirroring my sorrow and pain.

Mating

Other music we might hear from the dove: snap of sunflower seeds split into half. A heartbeat if we're pressing an ear to its breast. The mourning dove's unique mating call is hoo-hoo, hoo-hoo, hoo-hoo, uttered by males on land and only during a very specific season, usually spring. The sound is like unamplified back-up singing at a rock concert and, extending that analogy, their behavior like fans in the audience nodding their heads to the beat. The lovers preen each other with gentle nibbles around the neck, then progress to grasping beaks and synchronizing their bobbing. And once "married," they manifest fidelity well after the breeding. As long as they are alive. Hunters and predators take their toll, but don't feel sorry for them. Off they go in search of another mate, breeding like rabbits, sometimes six times a season. Studies show their extinction is among the "least cause for concern."

As I attempted sleep, was I the only one experiencing that interior screeching and sawing of anxiety, that orchestral clamor, what the Germans might call *Klangfarbenmelodie*.

My breathing too was broken like a bicycle chain unhitched from its gears, or an engine with a loose screw catapulting here and there. Why is it the wee small hours of the morning are so blaring, lonely, and attenuated? Did my sisters experience this too? Or did we again diverge, scattering into four distinct states of mind. The one in denial slept like a baby, another turned to sleeping pills, the youngest to running ten miles a day till her body fell into bed like a stone.

Song

We have a larynx to sing, lips and a tongue to form vowels and consonants. Birds have something special—a syrinx, situated at the fork between trachea and bronchi— each branch with vibrating tissues, each tube controlled by individual muscles. The mourning dove makes little use of this ingenious anatomical construction. But other birds can transition flawlessly from one song to the next or in some cases sing both songs at the same time. The true master is the wood thrush. If you happen one summer morning to be East of the Mississippi, in a damp deciduous forest with a dense shrub layer (and you are in luck), the thrush will begin its ethereal fluting—to me, more lovely than anything you'd find in an orchestra, music from an ancient well of shadow and water.

Though we have no syrinx, there are people who can sing as if they had one. There's the polyphonic overtone singing by Anna-Maria Hefele—part spirit, part bird, and the rest one well-practiced human. A normal singing voice contains multiple tones, which we hear as a single note. Unlike most of us, she's conscious of these multi-layers and can separate them out, splitting the sound into two: the root tone and the overtone. The effect is quite beautiful, like the song of some undiscovered creature deep inside a cave. At a funeral or memorial service, it might represent the music of transition, of passing from one kind of being to another.

A dove is nowhere near this talented. The male sits on a cooing perch sending forth the repetitive perchoo-oo-oo-o, perchoo-oo-oo-o. The music is discernable, distinct, but still throws people off. I thought it was the hooting of an owl. I'm sure it was an owl. And even when we've got the species right, we continue to imagine the dove is grieving, because we have once grieved, and this song is the universe reflecting our sadness. Its message is territorial—a significant stance, my branch, my nest, get back, stay off, stay out.

Culture

We humans are so anxious to make our mark on the world. We make a bird ours because we've seen it, named it, recorded it, and translated its song into human language. We put out seed and suet and the dove flies in for our pleasure. We are confident that we are helping it grow, and multiply. We band and track and accumulate data for years, so our ancestors will know what we know and do what we do. Then we shoot it for sport, adding another notch to our kill list and perhaps a meal, if we are up for it. We make up stories about the dove. Musicians, with their knack for recognizing patterns (shape, balance, repetition, and variation), have stolen the dove's utterances. Ottorino Respighi borrowed the perchoo for "La Columba," a section of his larger composition The Birds. And there's Prince, who in perhaps his most famous song, translates the dove's call into a brilliant lament of his own.

Who can blame them? This is what we do, as humans. We commandeer the colors, noises, structures, and smells of the natural world to suit our thoughts and creations and history. We take it one step further and lose our objectivity altogether, assigning human emotion to nonhuman behavior. When someone we love dies, devastation kicks in. And if other human connections are not available, these substitutions are somehow comforting. We do this because it allows us to remember, to belong, to feel less estranged from the natural world, though in fact we are not estranged, not actually distinct and separate, but inextricably members of, and tied to, the living world around us.

It's early spring: the onion grass is up in sloppy, scattered tufts and the red maple buds have just begun to poke the air like sharpened pencils. Condensation on my window forms a kind of ghost sickle. While the rest of the house sleeps, quiet and dark, the dove alights on an evergreen outside my bedroom, singing Ah-YOU-you-you-you. I'm grateful it's the first melody I hear, ever so tentative, preamble to *Klangfarben*—that crackling dawn bird chorus. I can relax. I allow myself to think that the bird in its sympathetic circular way sings for me, and I am listening to the music of my mother's voice.

"Be Dark Night," by Phosphorescent
(Matthew Houck)

Makes me think of vegetation. I see a pond framed by sycamores rooted in a kind of primordial slime. I see the road adjacent, where perhaps I am driving. Call it March, one of those transitional months when we've had it with damp and cold and lack of light. The peepers begin to stir, pricking the air like sleigh bells, wafting into my car window as I pull up. Now, the pond stretches to its fullest. The color is brown, like excrement or the clumped dirt of a fresh grave. There are seeds underneath that will blossom into duckweed, and seeds that will die and disappoint. There's rain pocking the mud, a scent of fresh meat released with each drop. Was I expecting a hallelujah chorus? Angels? On the contrary, most of the trees have lost their crowns. They sway—not like zombies exactly, though just as stiff. One of them clucks gently. Pause. Their funereal song begins, and against all expectations, it is beautiful.

Clearly, I've allowed far more than the music to seduce me. It's obvious how I've tinkered with this rendering. If I'm using my imagination, why omit the singer's thumping foot and invisible signal as his band chimes in? What has the song become but a hushed, dressed-up paragraph fashioned by a woman named Sarah? Later, I come across a photo of the album cover, cast in browns and gold, the singer bare-chested and backlit. So, yes, the man who calls himself Phosphorescent could be compared to the silhouette of a crownless tree. Also, his rain stick, with its watery cascade of pebbles, must have led me to those pockmarks in the mud. And further, wasn't there a particular evening when I drove the backroads to towards a village called Stonington? I may have stopped at the pond, lingered on its shore, inhaling the rot surround. And the wind, trees animated, canorous, despite their missing crowns.

Concerned that I might lose track of Houck's song, I paid my ninety-nine cents online so that I could refresh my memory, make sure the images I brought up held strong, even if the lyrics were barely audible, except on the page:

> *Dark night; meek and aligned*
> *Stones, tied; domes, light*
> *Be dark night*
> *Doe-tide; field, camera*
> *Ran, delight; stand, alive*
> *Be dark night*
> *All rise; speed and alight*
> *Speed and blind; be not bright*
> *Be dark night*

I love "doe-tide" and "stones tied," "meek and aligned"—linked loosely by sound yet shunning the pop-song path which these days boils down to three or four words and a pulsing bass. These lyrics are dense, and more mysterious. They don't necessarily scan in terms of meaning; "camera" comes out of nowhere. Though the fragments are appealing, they are the very opposite of loose and long lined. Together with instrumentation and voice they create a peculiar "thing."

While researching this essay, I met a woman named Katy who has synesthesia, a condition she's lived with all her life, even as a child. Like many synesthetes, she assumed everyone experienced this enhanced sensation until she was officially diagnosed a decade ago. To her, sound and visuals occur simultaneously. When she hears a loud noise—a motorcycle roaring by, a peppershaker falling on the floor, a car backfiring, or a slammed door—flashes of white streak across her view. When she listens to music, the visions are more complex. They may be in color or black and white. They don't erase what's physically there but appear to be projected on an interior screen or hovering at a fixed distance in space. Letters too present themselves in color, even gender—K is a green female; P is blue, "probably" lesbian; T is male, orange, and slightly delicate. Stranger still, if woken from sleep, figures from Katy's dreams are at once stamped inside her eyelids, as if she'd stared at the sun too long and a likeness now hangs before her. This brings to my admittedly catastrophic mind those Hiroshima victims nearest the atomic bomb explosion—instantly incinerated, the silhouettes of their bodies burned into cement and stone. But there is no bomb or even a match struck for Katy's experience; a random noise is enough.

I asked her to play "Be Dark Night" and tell me, as simply as possible, what she saw. Turns out, she's familiar with the band, even the album *Pride*, but usually skips over "Be Dark Night" because of the opening dissonance and "various disconcerting background sounds." Here's what she had to say:

"There are cones. Tubes—layers in some kind of ocean thing. More tubes, like Christmas wrapping tubes, and long sheets lying upon one another (these are the layers). They float in a large, dark, hollow space. I can see the ruptures produced by the percussion. There are shapes vibrating outward, like living, breathing parentheses. So sorry! I don't know how to pin this down! Some of the percussion is round like whole walnut shells. The last bits of percussion are like coriander seeds. Now the song is over."

Unlike the description that opens this essay, Katy's narration is a more direct route from sound to synapse to muscle to pen to page. Of course, her writerly impulse introduces some interesting particulars: percussive ruptures, walnut shells, coriander seeds, and yes, those Christmas wrapping tubes and cones, which conceivably derive from the song's stacked harmonics. I especially like the "living, breathing parentheses," a weird and wonderful visual.

But more to the point are the halting sentences with generalized nouns like "large spaces," "layers floating," and "shapes." They're a first effort—evidence she's struggling a little. Maybe it would make more sense to draw what she sees. Visual-to-visual? I've come across a few such depictions of synesthesia, and most were, for me, only slightly more revelatory, perhaps a little too Peter Max. And I like the difficulty she's having; she's never tried this and there's a childlike innocence to her description. Her heart is engaged, the mind bypassed. She even cries. Music offers Katy an enhanced version of the world, like a sheer robe or color floating on water. It was also an interference, such that she couldn't see things as they truly were.

Matthew Houck began his career in 2000 as the much grittier Fillup Shack, drawing comparisons to Will Oldham, Bob Dylan, and Iron and Wine. With the release of *A Hundred Times or More* in 2003, he transformed into Phosphorescent. Under any of his monikers, he's known to be reticent when talking about his music. I thought I'd take a chance to try to contact him anyway. There was an address on his website and amazingly his publicist returned my email almost immediately: "Sure, just send me the questions and I'll pass them along."

I tried to avoid the usual—Is the song autobiographical? Real or invented? Everyone wants to know the backstory, and most of these basics had been addressed in online interviews. Yes, he's originally from Alabama though his performing career began in 2001 at bars and cafes in Georgia. Right, he fronted the cost of his first release. He lived a rough life on the road—drinking, drugs, late nights, blurry mornings, broken relationships. Apart from a few vocal backups, the album was a solo project— his guitar, his tremulous tenor. As he asserted in Pitchfork: "It's impossible not to draw from your life—that's all you've got. Even your imagination is instructed by what you know." The statement could apply to a synesthete like Katy too. Her visions are beyond her control, but her effort to translate them depends entirely upon a world she's familiar with. A synesthete in Northern Greenland would draw on a completely different set of references. Katy focuses on objects that might be found in her kitchen, or a bedroom closet crowded with stuff.

And yet, there's often no A to B relationship between what musicians know and their compositions. Many of Phosphorecent's songs are mournful. "I don't feel like a sad wreck of a person," he says, "but I write from the perspective of a wreck of a person." When asked about a muse, he fishes for the right words. "It is a strange feeling. It's an emotional and physical feeling, and there's an element of doubt when you're doing it, because you know you're doing something above your ability." I mentioned Robert Frost's famous line: "Like a piece of ice on a hot stove the poem must ride on its own melting." Houck gave a kind of digital nod: "It is like that sometimes…and other times it can be very much an effort of labor or craft, but yeah, on the lucky ones you're just the referee firing the starting pistol, or the chemist dropping some unknown agent into a vial and hoping for the best."

Two professors at the University of Sussex—Julia Simner and Jamie Ward— have conducted numerous interviews for their research into the neurological and behavioral aspects of synesthesia. Katy's been a subject and participated in a lengthy multiple-choice questionnaire where she was asked to rank specific colors from one to ten and link them to emotions. She found it extremely tedious, but the mechanistic approach is deliberate and aims to suppress free association as much as possible.

Among other things, Simner and Ward noted that the syndrome occurs equally in men and women, that it appears to be genetic, that the colors their subjects see are precise, remain consistent over time, and don't obstruct what they are looking at. And it's not uncommon for synesthetes to find putting their visions into words difficult. With a grant from the Wellcome Trust, the researchers asked filmmaker Samantha Moore to create an animated documentary called *An Eyeful of Sound*. Moore combined strobe-like images with excerpts from the interviews. It is the most persuasive reproduction of synesthesia I've seen—a convincing mix of music, visuals, and language. Below are excerpts, spoken by the subjects while listening to music:

> *From the top…it's…just*
> *Can't think of the right word.*
> *It starts like that…*
> *I'd like to get a little bit of…*
> *And these go up…*
> *Well, no it's not, it's going from my right to my left.*
> *Almost, only much thicker than that.*
> *It's sort of…*
> *There's more than one color there.*
> *I like muted sounds like people walking.*
> *Not clippity, like high heels but softer shoes.*
> *There's a kind of music there.*
> *I feel it in my mouth…*

Language to these folks must seem a crude tool, rather like painting with a broom. Or, on a grander scale, scoring a full-orchestra symphony for a single instrument—flute or clarinet, for instance. So much is lost, though the transposition may be pleasing in itself. For the viewer of *Eyeful of Sound*, the animation gives these inchoate fragments a bit of life, with color and character.

Synesthesia is an expansion, or translation, of one sense to another—visuals occurring simultaneously with aurals, smells with textures, sounds that taste like something. Attempts to make these sensations public, failing to find the right words, results in a significant reduction of the experience. And writers can err by moving in the opposite direction, their words elaborate, overwritten, obscuring the experience itself.

Though Krishnamurti emphatically stated: "The description is not the described," description is one way for a writer to enter a poem. I once mentored a woman whose son had recently overdosed on heroin. She'd been writing a memoir and wanted to get this story down while it was still fresh. She also insisted on speaking it first, and it was clear she was still feeling its effects, flushing from the neck up, her speech rapid and sprinkled with swear words. She even pulled out a photograph, folded into her back pocket.

When I turned to her writing a few days later, the story was threadbare, beginning and ending at the hospital with a series of sprints through one blind corridor after another toward intensive care. She was just too stressed out to notice details, and afterward all she remembered were the stark basics: hallway, son, doctor—containers for feelings, not the sensations themselves. I wanted to praise and encourage her. But, sitting at my desk back home, without the particularities of this woman's story or the advantage of her physical presence, I had trouble finding anything to say.

Generalities can be defenses against the unbearable feelings that arise in such a situation. We use them because they distance pain, they cloak and soften it. What a writer does to bring back the event, to make it come sharply to life again in the reader, is describe the scene using perceptual details: the smells, sights, sounds, tastes, the tactile feel of reality. If you are to rebuild an experience so that the reader can be there too, there's value in sensory detail. This information is what formed the experience for the person at the center of it, and if written with precise observation and diction, the reader can live through it too, unmediated by abstraction. Memory inevitably thins out over time, even when a traumatic incident is involved. In the right kind of writing, the moment expands: unique and like no other. Emotion seeps in.

Synesthesia itself is not art, visual or otherwise. It is reflexive, one for one, instantaneous, directly in sync with perception. Its images are blatant, obvious, and mostly invariable. If a synesthete listens to "Be Dark Night," and sees a mud-colored roil and sprinkles of black, she may come up with an interesting association like Katy's walnut shells and coriander seeds. But researchers aren't looking for originality. They encourage her to deliver immediately "as natural a reaction" as possible. They don't want an interpretation. Katy's shapes and flashes of light that accompany her music are undeniable, so ingrained she rarely thinks about them. None of it is irritating or invasive, although her feelings may be heightened, as in her reaction to the song. She told me, "I would love to 'use' it, rely on it somehow for creative reasons. But I'm not in control."

I am interested in art, be it musical, literary, or visual and was eager to know how Phosphorescent came to compose this evocative piece. He began, of course, with silence, the musician's blank canvas. Then what happened? A random chord, whisper in the ear, or remnant of dream? Was he trying to reproduce a rustle in the bushes, bird-call, death rattle, or was there some other triggering event in his actual surroundings? Was he deliberately aiming for that bagpipe drone, so common at funerals? When did ornamentation enter the picture? How much was habit, invention, craft, or just plain talent? Were there other indie singers who might have influenced him? I often started a poem with a line that just "came to me, dropped from the air." If the line was interesting enough and it had a compelling rhythm, it would lead to more. I wouldn't be surprised if musicians work this way too.

Historically, music has been inspired by poems; poems have been spurred on by paintings, paintings provoked by music. The arts are altogether an incestuous bunch! Even architecture can be driven by songs—the Italian architect Federico Babina based some of his designs on tracks by Amy Winehouse and David Bowie, whose work also sparked an extraordinary tribute by the modern dance company, Complexions. I wonder too, if Houck accidentally taped the chorus's warm-up—that tentative throat clearing, shuffling of cymbal or microphone, like that idle tinny downbeat that shuffling of cymbal or microphone, like that idle tinny downbeat that opens Janis Joplin's "Summertime." Then decided he liked an imprecise launch. Something casual, drawing us into his living room with its ragged couch, coffee table, and ashtrays clogged with cigarettes.

It turned out Houck created his song in a specific place, way out in the Georgia woods. A friend of his lived in a converted stone mill-tower—a round, one-room structure right beside a waterfall. "I never met the owner, but it was apparent by the furnishings that she had lived a well-traveled life and had amassed a fairly large collection of hand drums and rattles and shakers and all sorts of handmade noise-making things from faraway places. I became enamored with these instruments, and they influenced and were featured heavily on the home-recordings I was making which became the album *Pride*. 'Be Dark Night' began as a sort of mystical tone poem or chant—just voice and percussion. I tried to be receptive to that and allow it to shape what I was making."

He believes in more than one-point, daylight consciousness. His compositions take place in a delicate and dangerous in-between space, one that may or may not deliver. This balancing act, the casting about, so essential to art, is difficult to explain. For instance, elements of Maya Lin's Vietnam wall—the darkness, heaviness, a gap in the earth, and the names of fallen soldiers—simply sat in her imagination percolating for a while before she specifically envisioned the structure. I don't pretend to understand the makings of sculpture or musical composition, but I do know poetry, and for me meticulous observation is essential for entering the work. Then, what follows then is an *unfocusing*, releasing that sense of control, and letting the chaos in. T.S. Eliot said, "When a poet's mind is perfectly equipped for its work, it is constantly amalgamating disparate experience..." As I grew as an artist, I craved that negative capability. My best work came from that source. It was like photographic paper floating in a chemical bath, slowly revealing an image, both easy and dangerous. I prayed it would last and suffered when it fell away.

There's plenty of mystery surrounding the artist's process and, thanks to researchers like Simner and Ward, fewer questions about synesthesia. But maybe the two have more in common than we think. They both integrate areas of the brain, though in biologically distinctive ways, such as memory and association. Both synesthete and artist inevitably draw from who they are unless they set out to copy someone else's work. What we can't explain is *why* a song elicits the vision of a pond in one person and Christmas tree wrappings in another. Speaking of that pond, is it really a *willed* association? Is any imagined thing under our control?

Houck is not a synesthete, but he maintains when the music is right, the physical world takes on an otherworldly character: "Not glowing or altered but something happens that imbues everything with a kind of holy weight. Even mundane objects radiate with it." I know what he means. And one could surmise that Houck does something similar to synesthesia: seeing and understanding perceptually, turning words into music, following sounds with lyrics.

Art involves a higher level of cognitive integration. Art has the capacity to translate, transform, and communicate subjective experience. Oh, how I envy the musician whose creations do this so quickly, traveling directly to the center of our emotions. Even a bad, sentimental song can get to us, but a bad, sentimental poem? Not likely. Our response to music is instinctive, almost animal-like. Look at Katy—after just a few minutes of listening, she's in tears. And isn't it true, we reencounter those feelings, recalling lyrics from long ago like none of the algebra or geography or penmanship lessons we endured. Vinyl—the medium that snatches musical vibrations from the air, retaining and engraving them onto a disc—has made a comeback, contributing to this nostalgic sensation. The experience is unmediated, sensual, in-the-moment, denotative. Whereas, language is connotative, a more complicated form of communication that must be reconfigured in the reader's mind, a system far more human than animal.

It is possible that we are all, as humans, somewhat synesthetic. Music can prompt other senses: visual, olfactory, kinesthetic, taste. Even the song of cicadas brings back distant summers, the smell of fresh cut grass, the tingle of Coke fizz. A shrill clarinet presages ketones in the breath of a dying person. A tender pianissimo raises, ever-so-slightly, the hairs on my forearms, then seems to slip right under the skin.

Let's settle into that tattered leather recliner. Put on headphones for the deepest pour-in. Slip the record *Pride* out of its jacket—little finger in the hole, thumb hooked on the edge. Center it on the turntable. Lift the tone arm and blow off the clumped dust on the needle. Drop it gently on the lead-in groove, wait for those pops and crackles, and then the first track.

Nestled between a cleared throat and a death rattle, the song transforms you, vaulting from heart to brain and back again, up to the popcorn ceiling and hammered tin roof, through the Japanese maple, Cyprus tree, and into the clouds with a flush of bird-wing exuberance. *And your very flesh shall be a great poem.*

✳

She'd worked with words most of her life, beginning with a small poem she composed at fifteen, near a Swiss *Wiese*, where skiers descended cutting wide turns through the snow and spray. *Snow waves,* she thought, *or sound waves?* and wrote that down. Hiking the switchbacks up from the valley where the village sat, she thought of a caduceus with its penultimate wings reaching into sky. Waiting for the *Autobus*, she stood over an ice-glazed puddle that, when she toed it, shattered, like brickle. This too became an early poem.

In college, her first mentor praised the little Swiss poem, but did not accept her into the advanced poetry workshop. And no wonder, the poems were clogged with abstractions and little detail. Darkness, Beauty, Happiness. She pined for a love affair with words but had no notion of what that meant, nor what makes a poem *live*, especially in the reader. Her second mentor took a chance on her, for he'd heard she was a good student. "Rescuing a Hedonist," was the first poem she shared in that workshop and then only timidly. It spoke of a fireman who creeps under the smoke haze, breaks down a door, and carries a drunk girl to safety. In that workshop with half a dozen truly talented poets, she inched closer to the real thing until she herself had ten strong poems. Which were sent off to the University of Iowa's MFA program, along with her application. Of the hundreds of applications submitted to the program, only fifty were selected, twenty-five in each genre, poetry and fiction. She was among the lucky ones who received funding too.

"*Amarilli, mia bella,*" by Giulio Caccini
Vocalist: Cecilia Bartoli

The story behind the song begins in pasture: a young maiden falls for a shepherd named Alteo, strong as Hercules and hotter than Apollo. Curiously, he doesn't notice the girl, though each time they pass each other on the rough path to the village, she smiles or waves or nods her head ever so sweetly. No, his gaze falls elsewhere for he loves only flowers and can be seen swooning, hovering over them on the hillside like an enormous bee. The shepherd will not consider the girl, any girl, unless she brings him an exquisite, utterly unique blossom. But our maiden has not found such a thing. She approaches the Oracle of Delphi who counsels, "*Become* what he desires the most—an exotic plant, taller than any other with a single hollow stalk crowned by blossoms. Drive a golden arrow into your chest. Your blood will flare—flamboyant petals in red or bright pink, a bloom never before seen in these parts—in this transformation you will achieve what you desire the most." She follows the Oracle's advice precisely—stands before Alteo on the path, forces a golden arrow into her breast until the change is complete. The shepherd is smitten and names the flower before him *Amaryllis*, a luscious sight in any garden, like fireworks or a sparkler held tightly in a toddler's hand on the Fourth of July. "Open up my heart," he declares. "See love written on the core!"

Cecilia sails into her song from its high D and cascades downwards, as if she wore a wing suit instead of concert frippery. Lower the volume ever so slightly and enter a kind of reverie where the waters fall not once or twice but four times, each sluicing a unique path. There is bounty—its texture like cream or expensive silk. Soon, a cloud passes, and the mood darkens to middle B, F, A, as if the singer is confessing, warning, pleading—all three under her breath—then lifts again towards high D. Once, twice, three times we hear the light tinkle of the flower's name. All those "R's" and "I's"! We hover over the whitecaps. There's the scent of anise, lemon, mint. The sky opens in a downpour of whole, half, and quarter notes, some of them settling on our forearms, again, dislodging the hairs ever so slightly. Bodiless swirl of an oar in the water. First coos of an infant, so delicate yet rich with affection and wonder. I *beg you love. Hear me. We are one, Amarilli.*

Composed in 1602 before the development of the pianoforte, the song is meant to be accompanied by lute. But here we have a Steinway grand respectfully guiding the singer to her sotto voce conclusion, its progress shy, like stockinged feet. Any music, including Cecilia's float across the final lyrics *Il mio amore* gives us the opportunity to summon our own visions, and language to render it, written or spoken. A listener hears *what she desires, what she is.*

This is not necessarily what the composer Giulio Caccini intended. He and his clutch of thinkers and musicians known as the Florentine Camerata were unhappy with the style of the period, which focused on pleasurable sounds rather than message, and therefore failed to elevate the moral life of the city's citizens. The group believed the ancients were most interested in *communicating* with their music. The lyrics had to be clear, not muddied by the excessive counterpoint typical of late Renaissance polyphony. *They* must come first in composition, speech creating the shape of the song. In this way, society would be improved.

What *is* the message of this song? Steady determination leads to success, though it may be hard-won. Pride has its consequences. Beauty rests in the eye (or heart) of the beholder. I doubt many consider symbolism while they are listening. Besides, if you don't comprehend Italian or the text is swallowed up by poor pronunciation, the melody must do all the communicating. The irony here is obvious: the music of *"Amarilli, mia bella"* is flat-out gorgeous—ascendant, emotionally potent. The sensory element outshines everything: cultural context, moral connotations—the progress of music over centuries. We can't get past the sound of it, nor do we want to. In his attempt to teach us a lesson and avoid the effects of pleasurable music, Cacinni has, in a way, failed. But, what a spectacular "failure."

Yet Caccini had a serious impact on musical history with the invention of monody, which today can be defined as:

1. A poem lamenting a person's death
2. An ode sung solo by an actor in a Greek tragedy
3. An emotional musical style with a single melodic line, usually accompanied by a single instrument.

His influential and historic collection, *Le noeve musiche*, contains a foreword, clarifying and defending the form, as well as its proper performance. He urged the singer to "declaim" or "speak in tones," with careful attention to the structure of the poem. His main point of pride in this new style was its ability to "move the affect (sic) of the soul." The songs were transcribed to virginal and sung widely even before publication and the book has been translated into numerous languages. Today, there are very few historical music anthologies without at the least one piece by Caccini.

Le noeve musiche, contains twelve madrigals and ten arias for solo performance and basso continuo, including "Amarilli," which is deceptively simple; the lyrics are sung from beginning to end, though the second passage is duplicated allowing the singer to accentuate the plea, *believe that I love you. I'll do anything for your love.* Then—the ethereal, ornamental close.

Non credio del mio cor
Dolce desio
D'eser tu l'amor mio?
Credilo pur
E se timor t'assale
Dubitar non ti vale
Aprimi il peto
E vedrai scrito in core
Amarilli Amarilli Amarilli
Il mio amore

Amaryllis, my beautiful one
Don't you believe me, of my heart's sweet desire
That you are my love?
Believe it, and if fears attack you
Of my love do not doubt.
Take this arrow, open my chest, and there you'll see written
Amaryllis, Amaryllis, Amaryllis
Is my love!

"*Amarilli mia bella*" doesn't wear thin with continual listening or bloat inside our brains until we sour and must break off the crush. It is one of many "art songs," frequently extracted from the grandiosity of opera to stand alone in an intimate address and, like most such songs, it's soaked with adoration or elegy, love and/or death, life in its most basic terms. *Amarilli* is music to close your eyes to, beginning with story, carried through unearthly melody, arousing a bevy of images in the mind. Listening, we have no choice but to dream.

Perhaps we need to make sure it's this particular piece, not Cecilia who has bewitched us. Is there a better soloist out there? Five sopranos perform an identical song, each with consummate technique, but if they are *interpreting*, their style differs. There's color—brightness, warmth, darkness, depth, clarity, brilliance. A full palette of vowels—"a" could be "aw" or "ah" depending upon how it's shaped and placed in the mouth. And there's dynamics—loud, soft, volume of air, intensity, tone. Ornamentation may be transcribed on the page, but there's room for going beyond these suggestions, with trills and flourishes that vary the verse or phrase. A singer *thinks* about the lyrics then creates an honest, matching sound. All of this in the service of clarifying her instrument, of sounding like *who she is*. In my amateur ears, Cecilia's consonants and vowels are fully sculpted, even the short "I" and "E." *She* leads the small ensemble of violin and cello, varying the tempo while the musicians maintain a respectful distance. During the second verse, her delivery turns almost conversational at full-volume chest voice. Finally, her coda is a kind of laryngeal rocking. And isn't this what Caccini had in mind? If ever we needed proof that music is three, even four-dimensional, it can be found here, deep inside this singer's throat, driven by breath, shaped by her vocal folds that, like sheer curtains between worlds that waft open and closed. In the diminuendo, she lifts and lengthens the phrase, and the sound fades and ultimately dies, the "little death" we all long for.

Lola speaks in a child-like voice meant for children who sing in a chorus at a private school for privileged children and indeed, this was her profession for many years. Occasionally, she offers lessons to adults. Her drawing room is dwarfed by a weathered baby grand, pitcher of water and tumbler perched atop the piano's music shelf. I wait in the garden room with its glass coffee table covered with travel magazines, plants, and perhaps two or three cookies on a vintage plate. She calls me in. Her excitement is palpable. Sometimes she even trembles, clutching her elbows as if otherwise she'd fly apart. I am *that special* today and can't help but soak it up: Lola is so incredibly charming.

There is little time for small talk, as she hands me water and urges me to drink. We begin with exercises. For starters, she says, straighten up. Imagine a thread through your body, pulling you towards the ceiling. This will increase the flow of air. Breathe with your lungs and diaphragm and above all, stay loose. Slacken your jaw and massage your cheeks. Rotate your shoulders and swing your arms. Now, the mouth: roll your "Rs" like the Italians. Try this with a consonant and a vowel *brrrro, brrrrra, brrrri*. For the throat, hum a partial scale, then a full scale. Do this while blowing raspberries, while singing the word "Ma." Imitate a siren. Start low then sweep up your voice, descend and sweep upwards again, this time a little higher. Now try holding your nose. Last of all: let's pretend you're zooming, whooping along a zip line, inches above a lazy green river.

I take a sip of water. Lola takes a sip of water. Room temperature. No ice. There's a stretch below middle F where I sing comfortably in what 13th century composers called *pectoris*, my chest voice—high tenor, low alto—why I stood between the two sections in college choirs. My hidden voice of little color. Tinge of the masculine though a long way short of those Broadway belters. Lola calls it "rough." She advises me to concentrate on *voce di testa*, my head voice, which feels like mounting a spiral staircase to the attic where the quarters are seriously close. Still, if I lighten up, I can reach high G, slide upwards to an F, sometimes three or four times in a song. I cup my tongue to open the passageway, stretch my jaw into a long O, raise my eyebrows and for a few lovely moments I sail over the high notes.

Another term for head voice is "falsetto" and these days, there are plenty of women who have it too. Whether male or female, there's a point at which a voice shifts gears while ascending a scale and it's the aim of vocal training is to render that transition as smoothly and consistently as possible. Two muscle groups control the vocal cords— the thyroarytenoids and the cricothyroids. The former relaxes the cords, the latter stretches them out. They work like violin strings where a higher pitch is produced when the strings are at their most thin and tight. Nothing matters as much as relaxation. Otherwise, surrounding musculature jumps to the task and even a forty-five-minute lesson with imbalance and excess tension will tire a beginner; make her unable to sing the desired notes at all.

I never expected singing to hurt so much. It was like so much else I did, aiming for precision by tensing up, constricting the wrong, not the right muscles. Vocal folds are about half the size of your eyelids. Tiny spasms marched up my left cheek to my eye, which then began to droop. No way to hit those notes and *not* resemble a pirate.

In warm-ups, Lola has discovered a less taxing way to do scales: begin ever so lightly in the higher octaves and descend. Otherwise, she explains, I'm pushing my chest voice up too high, straining all sorts of adjacent muscles and no wonder it's painful. She asks if I might have allergies. Should we turn off the air conditioner? Isn't the humidity awful? Better for your voice, though. Here, let's drink a little water, roll our shoulders, and shimmy all over.

We are reasonable people with reasonable expectations, though likely with an immoderate need to please. After all, what is art but a yearning to be loved, accepted, to leave something of yourself behind for those present and those to be born? Oh Lola, what can I do to satisfy *your* desires? Should I gesture with my hands? Am I courting? Pleading? Grieving? Shall I pretend to be Alteo and if so, why can't I use my chest voice? Tell me, which is the real me—the rough or the delicate? I've tried to imitate Cecilia as she closes her song, practicing at home while facing the fireplace with its above-the-mantel mirror. My teenage daughters freak. My husband drives off to the coffee shop. Three weeks into my lessons, the family forces me upstairs to an attic bedroom where, at their request, I shut both doors. Even then I can hear them moan with displeasure. For amateurs like me, the Italians invented a special word to describe the flat, narrow noise I make: *trillo caprino*, a goat's trill.

And yet, not long after Lola expected me to: I actually improve. The once-isolated phrases coalesce, the seams nearly unnoticeable. I've mastered the Italian and settled into an acceptable *Moderato affettuoso*. For sure, the penultimate trills won't hover, the notes clumped together, sticky in my throat. But I can focus on timing and shape and color—*crescendo*, *pianissimo*, the *poco ritard*, and *mezzo forte*. I would never submit to a recording or video or a performance with a real, live audience. I'm not capable of elevating or transforming the song, as Cecilia and other singers have done. But the distance between us has closed just a smidgen. Because I have toiled and experimented, even suffered with this song, it has marginally changed me. I can more clearly imagine *being* a professional: Cecilia or other singers or even vainglorious Alteo, grieving for his lost love. That is the great gift of participation. We feel the music internally, inching towards what we want the most: a vein in our hearts flowing with music.

The story behind the song offers a dark Dionysian (who was, after all, a deity of the underworld), an over-the-top scene, full of blood and emotional turmoil. I remember these dramatic feelings as a young person, when the hurt of a break-up seemed endless. That it was better to die than suffer the thought of being alone, humiliated, and unloved—for the rest of my life. Oh, adolescence!

There is one version of the myth that lands a softer ending: Amaryllis punctures her heart only once; the wound remains open, and tiny splashes of blood fall along the path to Alteo's house. Within each small stain, a flower blooms. Alteo is smitten, Amaryllis's injury heals, and all is well. But how many listeners will have the patience to unwrap the song's many layers—the vocalist's interpretation, the lyrics in Italian, the Italian lyrics translated into English. Further in, the lyrics interacting with the melody and finally the story that inspired the lyrics, a myth thoroughly of its time and rather unsuitable for our modern age. All this, just to discover that "*Amarilli*" is just a gruesome love story? Who would have imagined the beauty of a flower could wound, or even kill?

From that, we hold back.

✱

Her father was a lover of early, baroque, and classical music. Also, jazz, spirituals, and folk songs. Sundays in particular, the volume kept low, he sat on our living room loveseat, immersed in the *Washington Post* (never the *Star*—too conservative). It was the mid-sixties, and he was well known in the D.C. area as a "whiz kid," who rose quickly in the ranks of the national government: the Pentagon, HEW, and finally, founder of the Urban Institute (a nonprofit think tank). He was a generous provider, a strong swimmer, a birdwatcher with a very impressive life list. He often brought his youngest daughter along on birding trips through area parks and fields. Thanks to that influence, the girl went on to write a successful string of books about bird behavior, all published with major houses.

He was also a tinkerer. He built a harpsichord from a kit. While in traction for a slipped disc, he carved each leather plectrum himself, a daunting task, especially lying down. He put a speaker into an antique dry sink, cut a hole in the cabinet door, and covered it with gold and brown speaker fabric. Nearby was a bookcase with extra wide shelves for the phonograph. There was radio too, frequently set on WGMS-FM, the area's only classical station at the time. From here issued Monteverdi, Ockeghem, Mozart's Clarinet Quintets, Bach's Goldberg Variations, Handel, Saint-Saens, Gabriel Fauré, Brahms, but also Mahalia Jackson, Bill Evans, Leontyne Price, and Louis Armstrong. When he was at work, the kids took over with *their* kind of music: the Supremes, the Beatles, Beach Boys, Peter Paul and Mary, the Who, the Kinks. One day on the playground, she canvassed her friends with this question: Who is better, the Beatles or the Monkees? The vote went in favor of those flash-in-the-pan Monkees. Silly girls.

Hum

We do not speak of rapid wings, each stroke blurred by the next. We wonder what on earth is approaching—a hummingbird or carpenter bee. It is not *our* sound anyway and we are not in the position to judge.

For some, a hum is a private thing meant to accompany a task, such as dusting tabletops or washing windows. It's not necessarily domestic: we can photocopy while humming, cut hair, wait in line at the DMV, or stuff envelopes. A hum can be lumpy and off-key. It can impersonate a purr, which in a dog sometimes sounds like a growl. But there is no danger. Humming is natural—an artifact from our infancy when the universe had exactly the right amount of heartbeat and heat.

It is possible to record a hum. The pianist Glenn Gould hummed obsessively as he played the Goldberg Variations, and other pieces. Fortunately, technicians figured out a way to remove the sound—an irritant to many, an oddity to others, and an attraction to a very few. He was often asked why hum, his face just inches from the keyboard. He answered, "It's very difficult, and it's one of those centipede questions. You know Schoenberg once said that he would not willingly be asked by any of his composition students exactly why such-and-such a process served him well, because it was in danger of making him feel like that centipede who was asked in which order it moved its hundred legs, and afterwards he could move no legs at all…"

Some say Gould exhibited symptoms of Tourette's or Asperger's. He washed his hands in scalding water before each concert. He was finicky in his control over every aspect of the performance—which piano, the concert space, its temperature, his father's old worn-out chair set on blocks, the rug he required beneath his feet.

As she aged, my mother became a hummer: under her breath when anyone raised their voice. Humming while riding in an olive-green station wagon, packed to the brim with cacophonous family. Her hum was strange, a four-note loop—C major, F major, A major, B major, Rest. Repeat. Rest. Repeat. She tilted her chin back and forth ever so slightly, polite but insisting. Like foot tapping, hand rubbing, and later, picking at her cuticles till they bled. On the way north to Wisconsin, she followed road signs with a nod of her head, singsong, as if they were lyrics.

The hum was low key, yet a powerful thing. It replaced the words she meant to say, what order they came in. Better a hum than wandering up the street, as her own mother had in the dead of night, till someone called the police. The hum was a stay against chaos, a modest argument against death, legs she could be sure she could walk on. A blessing. Yes, there were times we plugged our ears, gently touched her shoulder, hoping she'd stop. It's the little things that get to you, though it was nothing, nothing compared to the lack of her, which is all we are left with now.

✳

In Iowa City, the hunt for housing was her first challenge. The right time to search (late May) was over. The lucky ones, who arrived early were settled in whitewashed clapboard three-story houses situated close to campus. But it was August, and the pickings were slim. She visited three so-called flats: one in the basement of a house, with two tiny transom windows to let in light. Another with a kitchen and stovetop covered by cigarette butts, the insulation drooping, the manager sketchy. Finally, she found a little, but acceptable two-room apartment on Muscatine Avenue with turquoise shag carpeting, a shared bath, convertible couch, and three over-energetic coeds in the rooms above her. They partied constantly, despite her pleas and objections. She can't recall ever turning out more than a handful of lines at her fifties' Formica kitchen table, so she set out to find quieter locations. There was nearly as much chatter at the library, so she tried working in coffee shops, airless attics, park benches. She turned to earplugs and a fan's white noise. But the problem persisted, and she never found that perfect place to write. In the end, a friend offered her sunporch overlooking a field full of weeds. She sat there in the quiet, stared and waited and waited and finally dropped a few words on the page, but it was obvious she was pulling from an extremely dry well. Alas, she was still fashioning a persona herself with no clue how to "find her voice."

Then, as an exercise, she wrote persona poems, imagining Louis Verendrye exploring a waterway to the West, or St. Clare on her deathbed, or the words of the Chinese Empress Dowager advising her husband the Emperor—*Like crazed horses the two-tongued/strangers advance. Come, edge closer.*

She went so far as to pretend she was writing, not as a woman, but in the guise of a man. Most of her models and teachers were men after all, and they were successful, weren't they? Their poems were published in prestigious places. In her soul, she knew she was lying.

Finally, a friend suggested she make it a goal to fill up one page, every single day. A nonchalance, like shaking water from an umbrella. Through this exercise, she began to shed her defaults and empty language. Slowly and surely, the noise slipped away. She cared less about the product than the process. The over-critical editor in her finally stepped back, freeing that much wilder self, the artist.

"The Four Seasons: Winter & Summer,"
by Antonio Vivaldi

"A song has a few rights the same as ordinary citizens...if it happens where humans cannot fly...to scale mountains that are not there, who shall stop it?"
– Charles Ives

As we well know, it's inevitable that some element of movie music will work its way into your heart whether you welcome it or not. In the documentary, *Mountain*, directed by Jennifer Peedom and narrated by Willem Dafoe, there are cuts from both "Winter" and "Summer" of *The Four Seasons*. It's the audio energy behind the otherwise near-silent shots of falling mountain climbers, ski jumpers, and snowboarders hurtling down slopes at enormous risk. I'd been waiting impatiently for this film because mountains obsess me, especially those youngsters with their Mohawk ridges and pitches so vertical no bird would consider perching, yet climbers do—some without ropes, equipped with the right shoes and just a sack of chalk in a fanny pack. Although we are perfectly secure on our couches or reclining theater seats, we get a taste of the terrible, enough to keep us coming back. Mountaineers, wing-suit flyers, high-elevation snowboarders, skiers, and other athletes experience terror and beauty literally; we do it figuratively.

In scenes featuring the most death-defying events, Vivaldi's concerti tear and skitter alongside. The effect is supernatural. The eye and ear are enriched at a polite and comfortable remove. We experience what Rousseau did, after a long off-piste hike in the Swiss Alps. "I must have torrents, rocks, pines, dead forest, mountains, rugged paths to go up and down, precipices beside me to frighten me, for the odd thing about my liking for precipitous places is that they make me giddy, and I enjoy this giddiness greatly, provided that I am safely placed." He neatly described the way most of us approach risk: with guardrails and professional guides and trail signage indicating both direction and distance.

For two years I lived in Switzerland. I was a teenager, hiking in the mountains numerous times and never really minding the signs. They were for old people (and there were many of those, grandmothers and grandfathers trekking well into their eighties). My friends, especially the boys, made the downhills a race, cutting through switchbacks, tripping over roots, righting themselves in a flash. No doubt they were just showing off, loving the thrill of stumbles and falls. Or did these hormonally charged kids have a death wish?

For athletes, however, especially those in the mountains, the only rapture is going way, way above your comfort level—challenging the law of gravity, flying up in its face, and hovering there even if that moment is ridiculously brief. The experience links two powerful sensations—fear and craving. The result can be triumphant or catastrophic. We wonder: once they've conquered their Seven Summits (Denali, Kilimanjaro, Aconcagua, Mount Elbrus, Mount Vinson, Puncak Jaya, Mount Kosciuszko, and especially Everest), will they keep going? Most likely.

My youth was full of unwise decisions—hopping across the moss-covered ledge of a twenty-foot waterfall, oblivious to the plunge pool below knotted with stones. Traversing a slope on skis, right up to the drop-off at the evergreens before setting my edges and turning. Mounting the steep trail to a glacier, determined to set foot on its ancient ice (especially the cornflower blue kind). I passed a barricade that warned, in three languages, not to proceed any further without an escort. I proceeded, got as far as the slippery moraine, slipped sideways, and then fortunately turned around. The excuse I told myself was the Swiss guard standing at the entrance, ready to give me a scolding. That would have been an embarrassment I couldn't afford.

Later in life, during several return visits, I appreciated the bright yellow trail markers, the well-groomed paths, and small benches placed at particularly breathtaking views. Still, there are cliffs and overhangs without protection, and I remember inching close to these drop-offs, my body madly signaling with bursts of adrenaline all the way to my fingertips, even my teeth. It wasn't fun exactly, that mixture of fear and pleasure, but the temptation to linger on the brink was more powerful than I expected.

The *Allegro non molto* of "Winter" begins with a dozen bright touches from the strings, a kind of ellipses that leads into an aerial view of two tiny tents clinging to an ice-encrusted near ninety-degree mountain face. To the right and rear, an avalanche blooms. From our standpoint it looks like milk in coffee, but it's more harbinger of the near catastrophes to come. All but one of the violins drops off and, as the soloist picks up speed, we watch things fall. First, huge chunks of ice break from a cornice above and crash around a climber clinging to his rope. Then come Vivaldi's descending scales and seven quick shots of other plummets. One man slips into mid-air from his handhold and slams back into the rock face when the rope catches. Another climber reaches for a sliver of shelf, misses, and careens to the right as if swung from a watch fob. His groan is audible when he too hits the wall. A third misjudges, skids, plunges, and somersaults at least twice, his body dragged back and forth against the granite and limestone. Close up, we note the ice crystals stuck around his mouth like salt on a margarita glass. Not a good day. He lifts his bloodied fingers to the camera. "Look what the mountain did to me," he seems to say in hurt and disbelief. Two fingernails fall into his hand.

Despite my teenage carelessness, despite the jumps into snow from a third-floor balcony, the drugs, the hash I hid in my purse at the border station between France and Switzerland, the wine we drank when the adults were sleeping, the sex we had in farmer's barns—I managed to avoid a serious catastrophe.

The catastrophe would come much later, when my husband purchased a bright red Vespa, (promptly stolen), and then a silver one. The two of us rode out to the country on that brand-new moped, a vehicle nowhere as sturdy as a motorcycle, much less a car. It was summer; we were in shorts, T-shirts, and helmets (thank God). We dipped and surged on the road beside the river, wound around several corners. And then, out of the blue, a wide sprinkling of gravel. The Vespa skidded and swerved, throwing my husband, breaking eighteen of his ribs, topping it off with body-length road rash, the scars of which he still carries today. My wounds weren't as serious though I had to push my front teeth back into place. I could hear him groaning fifteen feet away—crawled over to his now still body and jammed one finger into his shoulder to make sure he was alive. Oh, he was alive, all right. After an hour, the ambulance finally arrived. An

EMT strapped us onto backboards, guided us into the rear of the truck, and tore off our clothes from the waist up. That driver took off at full speed, making the ride almost as painful as the accident.

Two or three days after surgery, my husband contracted MRSA—so sick, so weakened and spongy, it took nearly a year for a full recovery. And yet, to him, in the strange twilight of violence to the body, it didn't seem like a horrible thing. He accepted it, ready to continue down the road to the very end, hands free.

The storms of "Summer" crash in, though we're far from balmy beaches, blossom-rich meadows, and leafy streets. Vivaldi's *Presto* opens with set of ominous staccatos by the violins, as we follow three miniscule figures up a snow-covered, forty-five-degree acute angle mountain flank, poles on their backs. The camera zeroes down. With each step the skiers sink to their knees. Their pace is glacial, especially as the camera again pulls back, revealing how far they must go. In a flash, they're descending through thigh high powder, accompanied by Vivaldi's flurry of short musical scales (what goes up must come down). The skiers swerve around close-set pine trees and boulders, tip backwards, execute flips. The landings look like so much fun—powder flying sky-high, somehow in sync with the *Presto's* accentuated notes. If Mozart's *Requiem* wrestles with death, then this Vivaldi, in some crazy way, *flirts* with death.

Dafoe rolls on: "As everyday life has become safe and more comfortable for some, we have begun to seek out danger, elsewhere." That "elsewhere" could be any mountainous area if the encounter is formidable. But this is movie time, and the music again picks up speed, as if someone adjusted the metronome for maximum punch. Hours pass at an unnatural rate. In less than a minute, a midnight sky speckled with stars morphs into dawn. Traffic on a looping mountain road is a mere blip of headlights, then a crazed blur. A parking lot fills up in a few seconds. T-bars whip by, carrying more skiers to the summit. And each gondola that passes is punctuated with a quick but forceful pulse—a signal that all this up and down action is unstoppable.

Death is certain. Music is intuitive, but where it leads is uncertain. We can be tempted by this uncertainty. I was a foolish kid, jumping into bottomless quarry pools, scrambling up talus slopes (high on mescalin), then balancing on a foot-wide trail at the tip of the *Brienzer Rothorn*. We were foolish adults, purchasing the bike in the first place. It was our first brush with mortality, and, in the end, we were darn lucky.

Over the coming eras, downed evergreens and scree will be replaced with other trees and pebbles. Icicles will melt and reform. Waterfalls and rivers will erode their boundaries or dry up completely. Mountain goats will evolve into hardier species or go extinct. Everest will grow a quarter inch every year, say geologists. If that seems like nothing, consider its age: 50 million to 60 million years old. A mountain may launch upwards from some place deep inside the earth, but weather's wear and tear will likely force them down again—an eons-old cycle that dramatically dwarfs the lifespan of a person. In this context, what proof of my existence might be lodged there, or anywhere? Whatever summit cap, crest, crown, lip, or ledge becomes the resting place for my ashes, whatever glossy sapphire lake or river bottom swallows them, they'll disappear in a flash.

She was drawn to poetry with a rolling kind of music, like Nicanor Parra and C.K. Williams. But given the assignment to write an extended narrative poem, she froze, unable to detach herself from the stark influences of Louise Glück and Laura Jensen. There was music in that too, of course. But her attempt to loosen up was a mere twenty-eight lines, the best she could do. In her workshop, each poet read aloud a long poem, and then listened quietly to the feedback. The rules were clear: no crosstalk, no excuses. After we imparted our criticism or praise, it was on to the next poem by the next poet. The last to share was Jorie Graham who presented a four-page, single-spaced narrative that mined her upbringing in Italy in detail—the art of dining with its serious stipulations for creating a feast and elegant table—to be consumed, of course, by the most highly esteemed company. She read the whole thing in her elegant clear voice, and when she finished, the group sat silent, completely stunned. Who could top that? Graham was a princess, a star, a visitor from another planet. Rumors circulated that she was allowed to skip the application process entirely. And she could afford to rent a two-bedroom apartment where she hung, with a few thumbtacks, an unframed, authentic Rothko.

"It was in the family," someone whispered. All of which contributed to the Iowa Workshop mystique. After all, Flannery O'Connor, John Berryman, Marilynne Robinson, Philip Roth, Louise Glück, Mona Van Duyn, Rita Dove, John Cheever, and so many other shining stars were also students there.

This writer wasn't alone in the jealousy and awe. At twenty-two, she just hadn't lived enough, hadn't discovered where her place was artistically so she swung all over the place—prose poems, sonnets, ghazals, acrostics, villanelles, three- and four-line aphorisms, one called "Casual Lies." The more condensed the better. This writer began to think of her work as miniatures. Not so unusual. Other writers just had larger canvases.

"Right Next Door (Because of Me)"
Vocalist: Robert Cray

The clue to an affair might be a balled-up pair of socks under the bed. Or an auburn hair in the bathroom sink. Even wet, it signals something. An argument too, overheard right through the wall of a motel makes the betrayal all too clear. There's always *some* evidence and those who jump thoughtlessly into an affair are generally not the meticulous kind. They like the risk and the conquest; the danger is at least half of the pleasure.

When I was eighteen, a certain Robert broke my heart. He said he'd pick me up by the little bridge and we'd drive the fifteen miles to Great Falls, crank up the radio, and walk the Billy Goat Trail. But Martha, lovely Martha was at the wheel. For years, her picture was thumbtacked to the wall above his pillow. I'd given him my photograph too, but never saw it again. News enough.

He was my first sexual experience, the longest relationship I had at the time (one year). I missed him so much: the stringy long hair, the dented teeth, the pale blue T-shirt, and Converse All Stars he wore down to a nub. The big old step van he painted red, white, and blue that we rode in all over town and into the forest where I went to sleep on his chest next to a blazing campfire. Martha and Robert took all that away from me without a heads-up or apology or even casual confession.

You can dream about affairs; you can visualize sex with any man or woman—in front of an open door or floor-to-ceiling windows or practice the irresistible come-on line, but none of this requires a confession. Your secret is safe. For me, it's still rather shocking: no one else was aware my Robert was having an affair with Martha, not his friends, my sister, or his mother. He wasn't into public displays of affection. Too risky, I suppose. I went off to college where, in my mourning, I searched for another Robert in the Kens and Alans and Christophers and Aarons and Stevens and Adams there. But it would be years…

Robert Cray chose to sing *Right Next Door (Because of Me)* and it got him into a little trouble. The lyrics describe a man listening through the flimsy walls of a motel to a couple deep into an argument. He realizes his affair with the woman in the adjacent room has caused their furious words, as he can hear her lover shout "unfaithful woman!" And who was responsible for this mess? The man himself, who admits to being a "strong persuader" but considers his affair to be "just another notch on his guitar." Unfortunately, the consequences lay heavily on the couple next door, their hearts utterly shattered. It was indeed, because of him, a "young buck" or, as Cray adds, a "young Bob."

Robert Cray's song is a full-out confession, which is one way music works to clear up a mystery—the lyrics tell the story and once recorded and broadcast, we tend to believe it. Yet, Cray swore he sang not of himself but of fellow band member, bass guitarist Richard Cousins, his inspiration for the song. In a performance video, introducing the song with an ironic smile, he asserted that Cousins was the cheat, and he wanted everyone to know that.

Later, he shifted the blame to his producers Bruce Bromberg and Dennis Walker, who also wrote his material. "Dennis Walker *was* 'Right Next Door,'" Cray adds "The song painted pictures like the porch light and sneaking around and being in your nightgown, and your secret's safe with me—all those things that Dennis Walker knew so well, having been married three times. And I love Dennis's songwriting because they did—they painted pictures. But I added the 'young Bob' in the song and now I'm associated with that, so that's kind of a hard thing to live down."

Musicians, like writers, can decide whether a song is autobiographical or fictional or someone else's story. He didn't have to add that Bob, but it might have been an unintended form of penitence.

In the end, I was the one to cut things off with my Robert. I wrote a Dear Robert letter. I wrote a Dear Robert letter to my dear Robert. Hurt comes first, then anger. I could think of no way to react, except to strike back. *Dear Robert, you could have told me directly. I didn't have to find out through your mother and your sister and the rest of your friends. You can't have it both ways. From now on, we are done.* Later I heard the letter made him very upset. He should have known it was coming. It was because of him.

Years passed; I met my husband. My husband had an affair. With me. In response, his then-wife put her foot through his guitar, another kind of revenge. He could have kept it secret, but my car, loaded with furniture and clothes and books pulled up in front of their apartment and that settled it for good.

A young buck is an alluring creature, sculpted by its Maker with vitality and innocence, unless you consider, as sin, the animal's drive to mate. We've heard many times before that sex and death are inexorably linked. The species is wired to reproduce, to guarantee offspring, which is an afterlife of sorts. But there are limits.

None of this drama seems to bother Cray's fans. And there were plenty. A pair of newlyweds headed down from Detroit to the Kentucky Derby. *Strong Persuader* was the only music they played in the car for five hours. A woman bought *Strong Persuader* at Tower Records in New Jersey. She loved it so much she burned through four cassettes. Another lived above the riverfront in Wheeling, West Virginia. In the park below her window, there was a blues fest featuring Robert Cray. She couldn't afford the tickets, so she lay on her bed and listened to his entire set, for free.

The song debuted in the eighties. It's timeless, some will say—actual music with lyrics for adults performed by people who used real guitars and drums, not digital sound machines. Right up there with B.B. King, Clapton, and Stevie Ray. Others will demur, insisting Cray's tone isn't gritty enough. "Balls to that," says my mate. But consider the woman who was wronged. She sits in traffic, hot as hell in her car, turns on the radio and out bursts "Right Next Door." She knows the truth of this song and must experience it again and again. A kind of curse.

No one should die with a secret. An admission of guilt can be likened to shedding objects from a hot air balloon—first the sandbags, then the raingear, then the basket you are riding in, tethers sliced with a hunting knife. You will feel weightless, like worn threads falling from the holes of a button.

There is one confession I'll never make, though I was only twenty-one and under the influence of a strong persuader. It was as close to "sin" as it gets. But was it cruel, greedy, spurious, illegal? Were there consequences, a pregnancy perhaps? I certainly won't be telling you. I'll take it to my grave.

✳

Back in Iowa, the MFA graduates celebrated with a lush, alcohol-soaked party. The women wore wrap-around skirts and skimpy blouses. They glued sequins to their chest and faces and sashayed around in flowy dresses. The men persuaded them all to form a line dance, and amazingly they obliged, nine women in the back, left legs raised, right arms seductively suspended in the air. Two on the floor in the curvy posture of water nymphs nestled into a fountain. They were the linguistically adept, body clumsy Rockettes! It was a drunken mess of a send-off; one they would never forget.

Most went on to publish books, earn major awards, and teaching jobs. One fellow figured an ad agency would be a better bet and scooted off to New York City. We renters said goodbye to our farmer landlord, whose name was...Art Colony. Because even the God they didn't believe in, had a sense of humor.

Her mother drove out to the country in a bright orange VW van ready to cart all her stuff back to Maryland, loading the van with poetry and fiction books, two rattan chairs, a couple of lamps, and a copy of her MFA thesis: "Common Territory." They stopped at a hotel halfway through Pennsylvania and swam in the tepid indoor pool, and she remembered with pleasure that her father wasn't the only one who excelled at swimming. His style emphasized strength. Her mother's style was leisurely, and far more graceful.

But after they arrived at the house, she knew something was off. The sisters were on a camping trip with their dad. In the kitchen, shoulders slumped at the sink, apron tie dangling, her mother turned to her daughter and said, "Oh, honey, I have some bad news. Your father has left us for another woman. Such a cliché. So thoughtless. And it's been going on for years. He'll be visiting with each of you girls to explain the situation in person." Suddenly, she was smoking. The daughters had never seen her smoking. Plenty of evidence—the cigarette butts in the toilet, ashes in the trash can. But rather than offering solace, embracing her mother, this daughter left the house, ran down the street, and sat hunched on a concrete culvert crying her eyes out—a real drama queen, hoping perhaps that some passerby would see her pain and offer a little comfort. She then headed down the block to her best friend Barbara's house, who pressed her: What happened? *What happened? Oh, divorce, she said, that's not so bad. I thought somebody died.*

*

What happens when someone you love receives a death sentence? First the phone calls to family, friends, and colleagues. The dozens of arrangements and visits with lawyers or doctors. All those signatures. Explaining the situation, again and again. Making sure the nervous ones know "you are okay." The nurse who clutched her mother's hands and all-out prayed to the Lord of Miracles.

Right away, the competition for her care began. The four daughters argued, and quickly turned mean: who will wash her hair this time, who make her soup, who write her goodbye notes. Jealousy when the youngest was called to read her favorite poems or sort through the albums to find some gentle music. Their mother refused any liquid, but for God's sakes, they had to keep the water fresh, a straw and extras in case she dropped one or tossed it away. Then the over-optimistic hospice nurse, "But you still have your hair!" (The chemo cut short at Mother's request.) Oh, that false hope; it was so cruel!

Then there was the well-meaning aunt who bustled in with a basket of herbs and creams and flowers. Pots of her beloved impatiens placed on the dresser. A brand-new radio so she could listen to NPR. A new nurse exclaiming, "But you still have your hair!" Then shared the story of another woman on her deathbed, who suddenly sat up, swung her legs onto the floor and walked across the room. "You must try a round of this miracle drug," she urged. "The miracle that brought back my friend's life!"

Their father on the phone begging to have a moment with his ex-wife because he loved her too. Would that be possible?

"Absolutely not," Mother exhorted, "No. He is gone to me."

The "Benedictus"
from Mozart's *Requiem*

Several decades ago, my cousin Nan and I snuck into one of the Kennedy Center Opera House's faux velvet box seats to witness our first performance of Mozart's majestic, heart-rending *Requiem* Mass. We were a little late, nervously keeping one eye out for the ushers. But as each section unfolded—the "Introit," "Kyrie," "Sequentia," "Offertorium," "Sanctus," "Benedictus," "Agnus Dei," and "Communio"—we turned to each other in giddy astonishment. "I can't believe we're hearing this for the first time. I don't know if I should cry or clap until the chandelier begins to shake. Are you feeling what I'm feeling?" Now, decades later, the arrival of another performance just a dozen miles from my home in Louisville, was almost too good to be true. The conductor Teddy Abrams had been called from Brooklyn to our fair city to lead the Louisville Orchestra, which had struggled with dwindling audiences and budget shortfalls for several years. He arrived with a superlative dossier, including orchestra stints in Budapest, Washington, Houston, Phoenix, Jacksonville, San Francisco, Vancouver, Indianapolis, Florida, Detroit, and many more prestigious occasions. When he took up his position in Louisville as conductor and musical director, he was just twenty-seven.

Whitney Hall is full to the brim, awash with murmurs and the rustling of programs, coats removed, purses stashed. Every seat is occupied, the stage and house glowing in shades of orange and red. The applause begins as the conductor steps up. He is all business—flicking his wrists with high precision, extending all ten of his fingers to signal a close, elbows forward and back in rapid succession. I've watched this conductor's gestures and seen chop, pierce, and sever. I thought of a baker mixing, whipping, and folding. Others have compared these motions to the crest, trough, and face of a wave. In any case, gesture is the thing when communicating artistic directions—with baton, forefinger, pinky, or thumb, both arms and whole body. It's a thrill to see Teddy—so utterly confident, leafing through his score as if he were reading an irresistible novel. Meanwhile, the choir members *et al* snap through their pages. From my seat in Row L, second balcony, it sounds like the rustle of bird wings.

Mozart was a divine master of melody, even as a child. According to family accounts, his compositions often began with a simple improvisation, composed in his head or on the piano. Then, under conscious control, he heaped on complicated variations and transformations. There might be three or four melodies going at once, each of them self-contained and complete. I never grow tired of those overlapping phrases, floating unbidden through my consciousness for decades. Mozart was a master of equilibrium, beautifully realized here, in the *Requiem*—its texture, tempo, dynamics, color, and of course, harmony.

For an annoying five minutes, my concentration is broken by a man seated next to me, slurping his bourbon from a clear plastic cup. T*ry listening with your eyes closed*, my husband says, okay. Inside, I see a featureless umber screen. No sparkling chandelier or elegant satin curtains. No enormous kettledrum or piano crowded into the center of the orchestra. Why am I here if not to watch the bows slide across the bellies of violins, violas, and cellos? And the orchestra dressed in black, perched on the edges of their chairs, their posture impeccable. Even when silent though, I can tell the music has been working inside them. The soprano nudges the air rhythmically, taps her sensible shoe along with the opening movements. The tenor stretches his jaw wide open, slowly shuts. The bearded bass might fit in well at a hipster coffee shop until he begins to sing. And what a sound he makes!

With reverence and wonder, we pass through the "Introit," "Sequentia," "Offertorium," "Sanctus." Then finally, finally, the passage I've been longing for.

The "Benedictus" is a breath of fresh air, a mellifluent break from the sorrow and angst of the funeral Mass. After the Sanctus, its "barbershop quartet" is the primary feature, cast in B♭ major, a key described by one of Mozart's contemporaries as "a quaint creature often dressed in the garment of night," her sound characterized by "cheerful love, clear conscience, and aspiration for a better world." Unlike much of the *Requiem*, which in its entirety can feel like music wrestling with death, the Benedictus is full of hope and reassurance that the Son of God has arrived. Even if you do not believe, why resist this sound traveling from beyond our knowing, landing as it did in the body of one particular genius—Johannes Chrysostomus Wolfgangus Theophilus Mozart. And what other musical phrase could follow this note than the Hosanna, a fugue picked up from the Sanctus, also in the bright key of B flat major? *Benedictus qui venit in nomine Domini!*

My urge to sing along is overwhelming. I experience the full effect, the "aesthetic chills" or *frisson*, beginning with my palms and migrating up my arms, my throat, my cervical spine, lower lip, and then my entire scalp. Miniscule muscles contract till my body hair stands erect, but just for a few seconds. Then the tears seep. I wish my art—writing—produced that reaction so directly, so effortlessly. Oh, to master an instrument as beautiful as the human voice or a flute, violin, cello. Musical instruments played for pleasure, praise, even money. (I wonder at what point a musician's performance might become merely work, a job.) Thankfully, I can settle for being a listener, and leave the music to the professionals.

It's the effect of great art, even on non-practitioners. We intuit excellence and intensity and desperately want to do it ourselves. As Saul Bellow said, "A writer is a reader moved to emulation." So true. We want to participate, create, leave behind some proof of our existence—the photograph that becomes a classic, the story collection that warrants a huge number of printings.

What I hear in the music is all too fleeting. Is there a way to absorb every single note, chord, phrase, gesture? If I followed my impulse and broke into song, my neighbor in front would not be pleased. So, I restrain myself, tap discreetly with right forefinger on one knee and begin a barely noticeable tick-tock of my head. It's enough: the luxury of the music pouring in, and the *dolce dolore* it carves in my chest once it is over.

Only a portion of Mozart's original score for the *Requiem* survives today. When you consider the fragility of paper it's not surprising. Much disappeared along with Mozart's death—lost or thrown away by his widow. One page was stolen from an exhibition at the 1958 World's Fair in Brussels. As you can see below, a corner is torn off that might contain the last words Mozart ever wrote: "Quam olim," his note from the

Introit to suggest the *Domine Jesu* fugue should be repeated. The ragged morsel of paper has never been found.

I played the piano for eight years, beginning at age seven, occasionally performing for a small group of parents and students in Mrs. Jacobson's backyard studio. What I remember most clearly are the Sara Lee brownies and Hawaiian Punch in paper cups laid out on her polished coffee table. Less fondly, the anxiety and constant practicing at our family's enormous upright. It took many days to master a short Sarabande from Bach's *French Suites*—the correct notes and fingering, then the phrasing, accents, and slurs. Once I had it down, I added color and feeling. I was particularly concerned about that feeling. Our living room was separated from the dining room by a pair of pocket doors; I wanted to be sure they were ajar and all four of my sisters were sufficiently moved as my performance steadily improved. At the very least, no one complained. But after Mrs. Jacobson passed away, another teacher took over, and wanted to hear the Sarabande for herself. After only a minute, she grabbed my right arm and said, "Oh, I'm sorry. That is *way* too schmaltzy. And it's *your* schmaltz, not the composer's intention." After that, my interest in piano lessons waned. A pity, too: I would inherit my father's harpsichord. But, after moving again and again, all my sheet music was lost, along with my desire to play.

Mozart's earliest sketches were just bits and pieces on a page—most of the music swimming in his head. Later he added the melody and perhaps a bass line. He then laid these scores aside as "finished compositions." Still later, he filled in the harmonies and many of the remaining notes. These, he called "written." If you look closely at the original score to the Benedictus, the basics are there, but not much else. Great swatches move along with little to suggest character. I could find mostly *tenuto*, only a snippet of *staccato*, and no accents at all—across all staves. But we are assured by the composer himself: "It is a mistake to think that the practice of my art has become easy to me. I assure you, dear friend, no one has given so much care to the study of composition as I. When I am completely myself, entirely alone...or during the night when I cannot sleep, it is on such occasions that my ideas flow best and most abundantly. Whence and how these ideas come I know not, nor can I force them." Any artist will recognize this truth. And most artists will have (at least modest) expectations of fame, praise, and money. While Mozart sank into poverty, his rival Salieri—a mediocre composer at best—was showered with lucrative court appointments and commissions. Mozart died at the youthful age of thirty-five, Salieri at seventy-four. Mozart's lifespan was just half of the one that Salieri lived. A ratio nearly identical to my mother's short life and my father's long one.

In the creative world not much has changed, except for the astronomical flock of hopeful authors furiously writing poetry, fiction, and essay. In turn, the number of submissions to publishers has skyrocketed. To this day, it may take decades for a highly promising poet or prose writer to surface, especially if the judges are considering factors other than talent in their reviews. Reason enough to return alone to that quiet room, and wait till the house settles in, the light dimmed, so we can focus on what is important—the words.

Back to the idea of a wave, which, in music, can be tied to more than the upswing and plunge of a baton. A wave has a crest and a trough, peaks and withdrawals, the wind in between stirring, nudging, heaving the water to its short-lived apogee. Then it crashes and the action begins again. It's a cycle across all life, whether ocean, planet, or human existence. Indeed, the smallest pieces of matter—particles—also behave as waves. Musicians make use of this pattern, this rhythm of erosion and lift, majors and minors, crises, and resolutions. Mozart's *Requiem* is cast in D minor, a key Christian Schubert characterized as "discontent, uneasiness, and gnashing of teeth." Tension leads to repose and stability, as well as a belief in the harmonious qualities of morality and the goodness of Nature. This movement from conflict to relief and back again is a classic gesture, a basic currency that occurs in all music, across art forms, cultures, and nations. Think of that floating place you call sleep and the morning that shatters it. Or a dream that chases you like a bear till someone nudges your shoulder and you're safe, back in your comfy bed.

While the composer was dying, his eldest son Karl stood by his bedside later writing in a surprisingly clinical manner, "...in my opinion his whole body became so swollen that the patient was unable to make the smallest movement. Moreover, there was stench, which reflected an internal disintegration which, after death, increased to the extent that an autopsy was impossible," (from Maynard Solomon's *Mozart: A Life*). Not exactly a flattering picture or kind send off.

Mozart died the fifth of December in 1791 at his home in Vienna. Of the exact details, there are accountings and re-accountings, versions, and one hundred and thirty-six post-mortem diagnoses:

He traveled to Prague to oversee his opera *La clemenza di Tito* and fell sick.

He told his wife he had been poisoned. There was fever, rash, and back pain.

When his health improved, he retracted the statement.

He suffered attacks of tonsilitis and strep.

That progressed to an acute nephritic syndrome.

When he returned to Vienna, he could barely lift a pen.

No, in his last two months, he completed *The Magic Flute*, the *Clarinet Concerto in A*, and began the *Requiem*.

He died of *hitziges Frieselfieber*, or acute miliary fever. Or Henoch-Schönlein purpura. Or he died suddenly.

Or he was well enough to invite friends to his bedside to sing sections of his *Requiem*. His breath must have been steady because he was still singing his Mass to Süssmayr.

In the end, he was buried in a "pauper's grave," a sentimental historian might say.

No, it was merely a "common grave," a pragmatic tradition at the time for anyone who wasn't aristocracy.

The weather was horrible—thunder, lightning, buckets of rain.

The weather was mild, with a slight mist.

Whatever the cause of his death, Mozart wrote the Requiem because music was his point of contact with life, mortality, and an understanding of what came after—his, the vision of the angelic choirs.

*

Not much left—some jewelry and clothing passed out among the sisters. A tiny looseleaf journal she kept, private and sad. She dares not look at what's written there. The photographs too: she's boxed them up for later, when ready again to look at her mother's face, whenever that might be. Now, she cannot avoid searching for her own face in her mother's face. *I'll be the next one to fall from our family tree.* Sooner or later in some cold, washed-out green examination room, a diagnosis will arrive, near-copy of hers, along with an estimated lifespan. There will be an announcement. It is news after all: *We are experiencing an epidemic: this is a fast-moving cancer. Monthly cervical checks. Bi-monthly colposcopes. Surgeries. For seven weeks, please do not engage in sex.* She bargained with God: *Give me five years, just enough time to have a couple of babies, the ones mother was waiting for, the two she would come to know, at least a little.* The nape of her neck felt warm, as if an animal were sniffing it. This was one way she grieved. This self-torture. No real measure of consolation.

"Black Is the Color of my True Love's Hair,"

Compact Jazz recording, 1989

Vocalist: Nina Simone

"Every instant is at once a giver and a plunderer."
– Gaston Bachelard

In 1980, my mother lay dying. I was twenty-six, my sisters twenty-four, twenty-two, eighteen, and thirteen, all of us shattered and completely unprepared. Her death that July guided me north to a high Victorian mansion in upstate New York called Yaddo and, within just three days, to my beloved. He too was mourning—his marriage a heap of burned and trampled things. When a *coup de foudre*, "cup of lightning," strikes two people simultaneously, surely the readiness to love came first. This might have been experienced as grief, a concavity so intense it sinks to all areas of the human heart, or quite simply an age-appropriate hormonal overflow. In any case, mind and body are in concert: Something must be done.

The mansion housed composers, writers, visual and fabric artists, sculptors, and more. There was a grand staircase, chapel, Tiffany mosaic and glass, lordly dining hall, and a cozy cocktail room with a mahogany sideboard serving as a kind of bar. Guests arrived, bottles in hand, most with the intention of sharing. Nina Simone's sultry, sorrowful ballad poured from a small boom box balanced on a chair. She was singing our song, but we did not know it was our song.

When my beloved walked in, I observed the following, through willfully rosy lenses:

His height, at least six-foot-three
His head of *black black black* hair
The purest eyes, wild-chicory blue
Clean-shaven jaw and chin
Cuffed shirt, top button open to a V, sleeves rolled up, those forearms
Khakis cinched with a fabric belt
Topsiders, no socks
The way he walked, soles down first, not the heels
The strongest hands, male-model perfect
Nails with milky white lunulae
Marlboro Lights and a bottle of Seagram's 7 he didn't share
Accent: New York, Long Island?
Great jokes, delivered flawlessly
So great, we all moved closer
No question, he would be adored
By someone

*

This is what he was thinking: *From the start, I felt at ease—safe, at home. I'm not sure exactly why. My animal attraction was strong. I loved her gestalt—a kind of smart-hippie-nerd vibe. I remember peasant skirts and Indian blouses and sandals. When she dressed in shorts, she resembled an awkward kid, which turned me on. I loved her hair: blonde, curly, and longer then. Her eyes were small and beady—I liked them. She'd read and loved the same poets and novelists I had. After years in business and my tortured relationship, it was a great relief and joy to chat about writing, especially with someone I was attracted to. Writing talk in that context is sexy and exhilarating. She was nondoctrinaire, surprising. She got my humor. A little later on, she belied the standard feminist credos by cooking me breakfast.*

The cocktail room also served as an intimate exhibition space. Poets and novelists read; artists cast slides against a makeshift screen. That evening, the room settled into darkness, and Nina was momentarily silenced. A journalist sitting to my right suddenly put his hand on my knee. "Is it my drink or are these paintings extraordinary?" he said. My beloved sat on my left, and he too slipped a hand into my lap—two offerings, one on each side. I have to tell you the journalist was not my sort of man, though a very fine man in his way. The phrase "in his way" had become a kind of practice for me, a nod of affection toward men who didn't suit my particular taste. As for my beloved, it was obvious at once we were made for each other. I felt sorry, then liberated.

Nina knew how to summon, as she said, "a state of grace," a feeling like "electricity hanging in the air...like mass hypnosis." Her breakthrough performance occurred in 1959 at the Town Hall theater on West Forty-Third Street, New York, a venue "for the people" that had launched or featured Isaac Stern, Marian Anderson, Rachmaninoff, and the bebop of Dizzy Gillespie and Charlie Parker. That night, the audience was filled with intellectuals, men in dinner jackets, bejeweled women, and various artists from the Village, all on their best behavior. The singer wore a white satin gown that draped over one shoulder and hugged her lower back. She was twenty-six. She opened with "Black Is the Color of My True Love's Hair."

Something in her magnetic, simmering voice makes it impossible to chat or read or anything else while listening. My arms go limp. Her arpeggios leap and politely recede. She fills the silences, but only just, as if we were napping and she wouldn't dare wake us. I'm returned to my mother running her fingers lightly over my arm. The rustle of sheets and purr of the humidifier and furnace stirring the air. I could sharpen that description, but I'd have to work at it. I'd have to turn the music off.

In the center of the mansion was a mock-Tudor, four-story granite, and limestone tower. Once, my beloved and I snuck up the narrow stairs, treading carefully, for the footing was precarious and we were trespassing. Not our given tower, not our daybed and wicker desk. Yes, we were writers, but not as famous as the playwright who alone deserved this magnificent space. Instead, we slept in smaller rooms: laundry room below mine, Ping-Pong table in play at all hours. His little cabin in the woods was like a screened-in porch, not very private, with a wood-burning stove, cot, chair, and desk, little else. At the enormous plate-glass windows etched with filigree and a poem or quote or dedication I can't recall, we watched light drain from the Norway pines and thought nothing of turning off the lamp, though it was not our lamp. We didn't care. Below lay a great lawn and, beyond, the fountain and the pool shaped like an infinity sign. There stood Aurora in white marble imported from Milan. Goddess of the dawn, garments flowing, arms raised in ballet's third, and by her feet an adoring lover. The other pedestals were empty, reserved I imagined for other goddesses and fools.

Our experiment in lust began. So incredibly fast—that mussing of hair, mashed lips, and scraping of teeth. My tongue with its aftertaste of spearmint gum. His breath sticky with tobacco or, wait...black licorice. Was that someone on the tower stairs?

In Fiji it's a sin to touch a person's hair but make him a lover and the taboo disappears. Oh, *black, black, black is the color...*

The French documentary *Nina Simone: La légende* opens in quivering vintage tones of black and white. We're inside a car rolling past graffiti-smeared row houses on a city street, and one of her songs is playing, a recording on cassette tape. Unmistakable, that damp sotto voce wail. The camera focuses on the singer seated in the back seat holding hands with Edney Whiteside, who was her first boyfriend forty years previous. He tries to comfort her, kneading her palm, but she is inconsolable. So many dashed expectations—lovers and two marriages, one lasting just a year, another a full decade; a daughter named Lisa, who would be separated from her mother for long periods of time. Nina regrets this and complains bitterly there's a grandchild she's never even seen. Once or twice, she chimes in with a lyric or two, but her heart is not up to it. "That, that's my music," she says, dabbing her eyes with a tissue, forehead creased. "I don't know what, what life is supposed to be anymore. I have sacrificed my whole life to do songs for this race of mine." Edney kneads harder and says, "Well, that's what you wanted, Eunice, and you were successful."

My lover and I left the mansion together in a 1979 VW Rabbit, drove to Norwalk, Connecticut, climbed two flights of stairs to an attic apartment he'd been living in for a year. On the first floor a gynecologist's office and, down the street, a chiropractor. Both turned out to be great conveniences (pregnancy, slipped disc). And the apartment! So snug, with 125 years of character! Recognizing something there, I surprised us both by weeping. Silly woman. The broken-tiled bathroom, kitchen with a pile of dirty dishes, bedroom in the middle but no place for a dresser, living room with a nook just large enough for my father's harpsichord. Could it be? It fit. We fit.

Here's what he thought: *She seemed to like it even more than I'd hoped. I didn't realize that the "me" details—like the printer's box with my boyhood knickknacks—would charm her. I see now that she was responding to a "me" that at that point I didn't think was worth much. The stupid polyester chair where we snorted coke, her first taste of bay scallops, then bay scallops covered in butter and herbs three times a week. The art-house cinema (that incredible short,* Harpies*). Just happy to think about the future for the first time in years. I had a weird confidence beginning in upstate New York that this was it, an absolutely right match. It was totally unexamined, instinctive, impulsive, and solid. Why I felt that, I really don't know.*

I didn't know I craved jazz or scallops or dental molding or porthole windows or even the polyester chair—garish red and purple—that unfolded into a ridiculously small bed. Love placed those details within me with amazing efficiency.

And there was more: I never exercised till I saw him swim. I didn't know that I didn't know how to relax until I watched him drag his lawn chair onto the beach, swivel his drink into the sand, lean back and gaze at the ocean for hours. He introduced me to the sonnet, acrostic, villanelle, sestina, and other forms. Ironically, it was an opened latch, a discipline that steered me away from years of modestly successful free verse.

He too discovered things, grew a taste for Mozart (though not quite exceeding his love of Bach). When they were still a bargain, he developed a systematic approach to outdoor antique shows: Begin in the middle and weave your way out to the more trafficked tables. His collections of Bakelite, samovars, toy ray guns, and fountain pens crowded the kitchen and filled our meager storage areas. *She civilized me, taught me the superior pleasures of staying home, of being true to my word, my family, myself. She pushed me to think of others (like my mom) when I'd rather not; demonstrated the value of steadiness, of doing the drill even when we don't feel like it, because it's the right thing to do. She showed me the morality of faithfulness to everyday duties, stopped my roaming eye, lassoed my roaming heart. She helped organize my life, changed all that I was into everything I am.*

Don't ask me to stop the dark spilling from this song. I chose it for that. We listened to other music in that apartment: Sinatra's "Mood Indigo," Mozart's *Requiem* Mass, Holiday. But nothing came close to the plangent dignity in Nina's throat. She was the High Priestess of Soul; she owned the song, stripped it down to its melancholic basics. She knew how to unwrap a chord, slowly, a woman distracted, mired in her thoughts. Her *black* travels a long distance before it becomes the color of her *true love's hair*. Her purest rings out in the dark, suspended before settling on *eyes*. In Nina's song, it's the modifiers that roam: pure, true, black. I care little that John Jacob Niles discovered it and rewrote the melody, that a Mrs. Lizzie Roberts first recorded it in 1916. Their versions seem frilly by comparison.

Here's what Nina leaves out:

The winter's passed and the leaves are green,
The time is passed that we have seen....
I go to the Clyde for to mourn and weep,
But satisfied I never could sleep.
I'll write to you a few short lines,
I'll suffer death ten thousand times.
So fare you well, my own true love.
The time has passed, but I wish you well.

The Clyde is a river running through Glasgow, proof that the song originated in Scotland, not Appalachia. I think it telling Nina deemed these lines unnecessary. She stops short of the well-worn Romantic tradition, the lover placed on a pedestal like a vase of flowers, the lonesome one reaching, reaching, unable to touch. With gaps and pauses, she focuses instead on the mystery, exploring that *Zwischenraum*, or space between things, where longing and defeat intermingle. Love's door, she seems to say, is hinged with pain, a lament that spreads across so many of her other works: "The Other Woman," "*Ne me quitte pas*," "I Loves You, Porgy," "Don't Let Me Be Misunderstood," even the sexy songs, like "I Want a Little Sugar in My Bowl." These, in particular, we couldn't leave alone. We'd listen to the point of irritation, then two weeks later listen again.

Here's a photograph: I'm in the tower, leaning against a wall, the window casting lacteal light. Through his lens, I'm ever so slightly blurred, cross-ankled like the goddess of dawn in her shallow pool. My *face so soft and wondrous fair*. That blurred. Nothing on but two Band-Aids stuck to my heels. Underneath, skin rubbed raw from a strappy pair of sandals. I remember those blisters—worth the pretty sandals, worth the pain if this man turns out to be *the one*.

He *was* the one, the two of us delighted at how we said the very things the other was thinking, sometimes in unison. In Venice, consuming half our honeymoon budget on a gondola ride and curried sole at Harry's Bar. Riding like oversize teddy bears on a Vespa, simultaneously blind to the dangers of grass shavings and stray gravel. We were both firstlings, loaded down with parental expectations but happy to defy them. We favored indie movies, indie bookstores, mom-and-pop diners before they were trendy. We read Nabokov, Renata Adler, Maxine Hong Kingston, Marilynne Robinson, Chandler, James Baldwin, Ian McEwan, Fitzgerald, and Hardwick. We were jealous of each other, but only in one area—solitude, time for writing. Even now, I keep my laptop screen tilted so that he can't see I'm finishing up an essay. As if I were reading pornography. Do they make plain brown wrappers for laptops?

Some people look at a long marriage and think: Those two are amazing. They match, like Queen Anne chairs. Surely, they have their problems—disagreements, false hopes (of course he'll change)—but somehow, they've figured it out. Life inside their dwelling is calm and respectful. One says, "Please tickle the fire," and the other laughs. It's such blatant code. She tolerates his restlessness, and he her lack of adventure. They memorize the steps, avoid the slick spots, pause, consider, and trust.

And yet, how quickly we uncover and probe each other's faults, rarely examining our own. Not long before we discover what drew us together, what was thought was a lit forest, was partly deciduous. We grow into street angels, house devils, charming our students and nagging our children. We aspire to human decency. Then, while arguing, throw a pitcher or pot of rice, denting the drywall.

Long ago, Mary Kate Waymon stood in their North Carolina living room and "almost died on the spot" as she watched her two-and-a-half-year-old, then Eunice, climb up on the piano bench, put her little hands on the keyboard, and punch out a favorite hymn, "God Be with You till We Meet Again." Music was in her genes; the entire family was gifted in piano, harmonica, guitar, and singing. Still, this toddler was something else entirely. She taught herself to play by ear; it wasn't long before she opened the service in her mother's Methodist church. At the age of six she was studying Bach with Muriel Mazzanovich (Miz Mazzy)—a highly authoritative yet courteous Englishwoman in town—the year of classical lessons paid for by Mary Kate's employer. Later, the small community of Tryon raised funds to send her to Juilliard with the aim of readying her to become a concert pianist. Nina suffered her first real disappointment when her application to Philadelphia's Curtis Institute of Music was rejected, despite a positive response to her performance. It was a decision she swore was based on her race. Instead, she took on students and, to supplement her income, answered a call for an audition at an Atlantic City bar. She was signed immediately, the owner insisting she add vocals to her brilliant piano. She killed it. Her reputation spread like fire up and down the East Coast.

During the sixties, Nina's compositions were outspoken in their opposition to racism. She joined the civil rights and Black Power movements, marched alongside Martin Luther King Jr., and performed during fundraising events and demonstrations. "Mississippi Goddam," "Four Women," "Backlash Blues," and "To Be Young, Gifted, and Black" were written during this period and inspired other musicians, including Aretha Franklin and Patti LaBelle, and later John Legend, Mary J. Blige, Alicia Keys, and others. The singer saw herself as a griot—that deeply respected West African minstrel who sees and hears and knows everything in a village.

Nina was a champion for "my people" but looked down on her black audiences. She beat up white audiences too, disdaining them while covering their popular songs. She grew demanding and difficult, the result of discrimination, financial turmoil, over-controlling managers, and: a diagnosis of bipolar disease. A bodyguard was once hired to protect *fans* from the singer. "I will never be your clown," she chastised a nightclub audience in Cannes for resisting a sing-along, then trudged through her set, closing with "I don't wear a painted smile on my face, like Louis Armstrong...I am not here just to entertain you. How can I be alive when you are so dead?" This behavior came to dominate the idea of Nina—irregular, unwelcoming. Critical work about her now has titles like *What Happened, Miss Simone? Princess Noire: The Tumultuous Reign of Nina Simone*, and *I Don't Trust You Anymore*.

Years passed. I learned a lot—how, in his mind, the language of physics and theology and the intricate world of a sestina coexist with random bursts of basso profundo: *Climb every mountain, forge every sea.* Or how the hypnotic rhythms of Arvo Pärt can be spliced in with *Bucky bucky beaver, bucky bucky beaver,* a 1950s toothpaste jingle. I realized he was a person of lifelong hyper-attenuation. A supermarket paralyzes because there is too much going on visually and spatially. Facing an aisle stacked with cereal, he ends up not seeing anything, forgetting what he came for. I tolerated his habit of throwing tissues on the floor till they formed bacterial mulch around his favorite chair. "Okay, honey," he often said, out of the blue, a signal like the game of Marco Polo or perhaps the marker of the end of one activity (sitting) and the beginning of another (standing). It wasn't long before I picked up the practice—an endearment that implied, *I'm fine, I see you,* won't ever leave you—whether he was present or not.

Unlike Nina, we suffered no serious mental illness, though the course of a year might include patches of resentment, depression, anxiety, and irritation. *She can't sit still. She gets up from the couch every five minutes to tend to something. She believes this makes her thin, keeps her joints lubricated—a person of industry. But it is difficult for me to function when there's a lot of movement around me; my brain is so perpetually awhirl that it makes me feel confused, fractured. I'm trying to get her to relax, to break some of her own rules, for life-affirming purposes. But I also admire her stringencies, because they have in a large sense allowed her to be/become so accomplished, as well as to handle the day-to-day necessities. So I am in a way envious, simultaneously taking it as my mission to show her how to give in to pleasure, over and above obligation. This seems more of the essential yin-yang of our relationship, differences that both compliment and mystify the other. We maintain an essentially harmless low-grade state of continuous warfare. Not a bad description of human relations in general.*

There are couples that are slow to trust, waiting years before moving in with each other, years before marrying, then a decade before settling on a child or two. We didn't require a trial period. We were of the same mind, held together by a habit of risk-taking and the willingness to go all in. On the honeymoon in Venice, we threw away the birth control and returned to the States two weeks pregnant. On a long drive back from New Hampshire, we stopped for an overnight in Pennsylvania—hound dog curled on the floor, daughters asleep in one queen-size bed, and inches away, their parents rocking and sighing with…perhaps…the idea of a third child. It wasn't to be. But the modernist house we fell in love with, well beyond our means? With three minutes to deliberate and a little extra work, we managed to swing that. I would be remiss if I didn't mention the consequences. One summer night, we rode the Vespa to a restaurant on the river, clad only in shorts, sandals, T-shirts, and, thankfully, our helmets. One sharp turn and we were down at forty-five miles per hour. I fell face first, road rash from my forehead to mangled big toe. He must have bounced off the chassis, shattering his ribs in eighteen places before landing unconscious on the asphalt. An operation removed the blood from his chest and lungs but introduced a dangerous hospital infection requiring IV antibiotics and months of recovery. It was nearly fatal.

Finally, as if to ironically underscore family togetherness, we passed risk-taking down to our children, along with the gene for alcoholism. The family that's sober together stays together, and alive.

I've never seen Nina perform. I was too young during the fifties when she focused on old standards, and I was mostly oblivious during the sixties, when her work became overtly political. Or perhaps I should say I've seen her perform only on film. Either way, I believe she came into my life at the right moment, when I understood no love is without its shadows: brief periods of discord, longer stretches of mishaps and stumbling. (So certain I'd marry a blond, but his hair was black.)

Isn't it worth asking why so many of us migrate towards darkness in our musical preferences? Because we are preparing ourselves for the inevitable, ready with acceptance when that diagnosis comes rolling in? I've always considered darkness to be deeper and richer than happiness. I can do without tap-dancing tunes, marching bands, jigs, and variations on Happy Birthday. Happiness floats on a thin scrim, easily perforated. This is why twilight is my favorite time of day with its silhouettes of trees, black against a salmon-pink sky. It's the promise of rest. Darkness is complicated, difficult to navigate, but in the end, it might be a safe place—our rest, our home.

In the *Compact Jazz* recording, Nina sounds exhausted. Or (again) is she merely taking her time, the opening arpeggio savored as before a ten-course meal—

that attenuated *blaaaaaaack* and mesmerizing *colorrrrr, hairrrrrr*? A flutter in her vowels, and hiss, a kind of shushing without the mean. I've tried to sing along but my voice sounds like skim milk. I rush the lyrics and interrupt her silences. I forget she sits on her chords till their vibrations fade. My melancholy is real, but no match for hers. She tilts her head to the side, not looking at anything, not the audience, not her manager hovering in the wings, not even her fingers on the piano keys. Oh please, she seems to say, just let me sing and get through the story of my true love's hair, of my true love's hair, of my true love's hair.

To close, Nina resolves to a major key. It may be an attempt to oblige the audience, to lift the mood. *All shall be well,* we might be thinking, despite the time spent in a minor key. *All manner of things shall be well.*

"Dancing on the Ceiling,"
from *You Better Go Now*
Vocalist: Jeri Southern

"For those who tread lightly enough the air is a stair." – James Richardson

The world is lyrical
Because a miracle
Has brought my lover to me
Though he's some other place, his face I see...

In 1930, the famous duo Richard Rodgers and Lorenz Hart teamed up to write this tune for a musical called *Ever Green*. Its premier performance occurred in London at the Adelphi Theatre, starring the dancer, Jessie Matthews. It ran for 254 performances, a huge critical and financial success that secured Matthews's stage and film career for years to come. In a daring move, the show took place on a revolving platform, a first for the city. The most striking prop was a gigantic topsy-turvy chandelier fastened to the floor (theoretically the ceiling), around which Matthews and her partner danced. Tiny lights, meant to be stars from heaven, whirled about them.

He dances overhead
On the ceiling near my bed
In my sight
Through the night

From the 1934 movie musical *Ever Green*, "Dancing on the Ceiling," a Rodgers and Hart standard.

As a child I loved considering the world this way—flopping my head backwards to scrutinize the upended chairs and carpeted ceilings. In my stifling third-story bedroom, I lay spread eagle atop the covers, sweat pooling in my arm and knee pockets. I longed for the cool of the basement where my sisters slept, so I envisioned turning the house bottom-side up till the desk hung by its feet and the three window eaves became a trio of foothills. To enter, I stepped over the doorframe and slid on my butt down the paint-slick surface. Leaving the bedroom, I'd scramble back up, barefoot on all fours, angling for purchase. The eaves took up nearly all the (now) floor space. Come to think of it, there wasn't even enough room for a bed; to sleep I quartered my bedspread, fluffed my pillow, and curled into a fetal position. This was acceptable if it was cool. Naturally my friends would be lining up to spend the night and romp in my playground.

A downside-up way of living was no stretch for this dreamer. Yet not all my imaginings were sweet. There were squirrels on the porch that transformed into burglars and kidnappers. These villains climbed the adjacent Scotch pine, branch-by-branch, rope, and pistol in hand, determined to break in and inflict some awful damage. Occasionally, a man (or was it a ghost) wrapped in a yellow sheet hovered outside the window. I built up the courage to tell my mother and she said not to worry, the idea was ridiculous.

> *I try to hide in vain*
> *Underneath my counterpane*
> *There's my love*
> *Up above*

I'm not a fan of the Jessie Matthews recording. It's very much of its time, pert and briskly delivered, the voice a little too *trémula*. Luckily, the song has made its way onto albums by Frank Sinatra, Jo Stafford, Ella Fitzgerald, George Shearing, Chet Baker, Barbara Cook, Jack Jones, June Christy, and Royce Campbell, to name just a few. For a while, I clung to Sinatra's rendition from *In the Wee Small Hours* for its winsome despondency. Then I happened upon Southern's album *You'd Better Go Now*.

There is something smoky and understated in her singing. The lyrics play out smoothly, even listlessly, one could say. She's in the middle of a lucid dream and for now it could be true: the man shuffling on the ceiling is her one and only. The man on the ceiling will soon be at her door. He'll take her in his arms and press her to his chest. But first he must practice.

The tempo too is just right: there's a kind of lingering expectation, but also acquiescence. Southern's "Dancing on the Ceiling" is a classic torch song, derived from the expression "carry the torch" for a man or woman pining for a lost lover. The singer's plea is sentimental and unrealistic, yes. Nevertheless, we find ourselves hoping she gets her wish.

Once, sitting under a backyard tree, my eye on a leafless branch just above, I beheld a sudden movement—not the swaying kind the wind inflicts, for there was no wind. No, this action was more articulate and independent of the twig. In fact, it was a dun-colored insect, very much alive. A baby walking stick! All legs and knobby joints, antennae waving like miniature searchlights. Its appearance was so abrupt, so unsettling, I felt sure the creature dropped unwittingly from an adjacent world, some heretofore hidden land of spirits.

Is the line between dream and wakefulness so narrow we can ride the edge of it, glide to and fro like water striders, another species of boundary skaters? These nimble creatures are also known as Jesus bugs, and surface tension is the reason they don't fall in. But a single child with an exploratory stick can change all that, break the spell with one sharp poke, forcing seepage between air and water, life and death. Of course, this is exactly what children do.

A door opens up. The bug slides in.

Edge territories—a lake's surface, twilight, sunset, falling asleep and waking up—are often seen as spiritual. They might stem from a drug-induced state of mind, or nightmare visitations so vivid they stick with you all day. They can be part of the landscape, like the vine-tangled banks of forest streams, shorelines, estuaries—any area where two biomes overlap. Or it's a particularly sacred spot like Skellig Michael, founded in the early sixth century as a monastic retreat. The island is forty plus acres of exposed, craggy rock, with precipitous steps carved into the cliffs—a dangerous undertaking no doubt aided by the conviction that each embedded rock lifted the monks closer to God. Today, it's a destination for pilgrimages, where it may be possible to catch a glimpse of the divine.

> *I whisper, "Go away, my lover*
> *It's not fair."*
> *But I'm so grateful to discover*
> *He's still there*

In this ballad, we get the strong impression the singer herself has stepped through the looking glass, into an empty ballroom lit by candlelight with high ceilings and the saccharine scent of lilacs. She is convinced her debonair dancer is waiting patiently for her appearance, ready to show off his—now fluid—dancing moves. Not 'sort of' there, but *there*.

*

Jeri Southern began life as Genevieve Hering in 1926 and, by age six, was well into her journey as a classical pianist, adding voice lessons as a teenager at the Notre Dame Academy in Omaha, Nebraska. She toured with a Navy recruiting group, and later moved to Chicago to work at various clubs and bars, where she was noticed and signed by Decca Records. Post-WWII, a slew of female jazz singers came to the fore, including Peggy Lee and Anita O'Day. But Southern suffered from overwhelming stage fright. Her own daughter had to carefully approach her mother's practice room and open it just a crack to catch her Debussy and Beethoven sonatas. The singer grew fearful even when she saw her name on a marquee. This explains her early retirement and part of the reason she isn't better known today. But Frank Sinatra was one of her greatest fans. One day, when they finally met, he embraced her to the point of pain, and whispered that she, she, she was "the very best."

*

If heaven is a looking glass, a reversal of our lives on Earth, would I be granted the ability to dance? Since no one knows for certain, we are each allowed to imagine a paradise of our own. My earthly body is wooden—inflexible even as a child. Watching me at the barre, unable to hook my heel on the rail without excruciating pain, my ballet teacher gave up and refunded my parents' money. But oh, to watch the yoga instructor climb a wall, balanced on her head. And, after their performance, modern dancers chilling at a reception, their supernatural gait and gorgeous caper blooming while the reggae band warms up. I'd like to be born again with that. And after we die, what if each element of Earth and mind were inverted? We'd have answers before we were aware of the questions. Mysteries would begin with resolutions. The peak of a dancer's career might trigger a long decline eventually leading to little hops and skips in ballet slippers and the very first steps she took as a toddler. There ought to be sun and moonlight, unimpeded by humidity and air pollution. Then maybe, even without corrective lenses or telescopes, we'd see across eternity to other universes. We'd witness the birth of stars. And decipher the thoughts of newborns.

C.S. Lewis visualized the afterlife another way. His book *The Great Divorce* describes a journey that commences with boarding a bus. It's no ordinary vehicle. The light inside is "blazing" and "golden." The driver too seems touched by this holy emanation and "use(s) only one hand to drive with." Additional passengers disembark one by one and wander into the landscape. Lewis writes: "Now that they were in the light, they were transparent—fully transparent when they stood between me and it, smudgy and imperfectly opaque when they stood in the shadow of some tree. They were in fact ghosts: man-shaped stains brightness of that air…"

There's no hurt borne by these convictions, no damage done to a poet or theologian or the woman in Rodgers's song, asserting with all her heart that her lover frolics overhead. Her notions are a private matter, dreams that please and console, that make her feel less lonely.

The world is lyrical
Because a miracle
Has brought my lover to me
Though he's some other place, his face I see

Any song or life is linked to heartbeat and breath. When a body fails and ultimately disintegrates, it moves on to other lives: the microorganisms in flesh and bone become food for worms; the worms, food for robins; the robins a meal for red-tailed hawks. And that is not even to mention the trees—Bristlecone pine, Sequoia, or Redwood—that feed on decayed matter, that can live for fifteen hundred years before passing their remains on to some other species.

Mary Oliver imagines death as a re-arrangement of our atoms, the way a sprig will sometimes rise from a scorched field. Animals continue to adjust and evolve. The monk and poet Paul Quenon disagrees with Oliver, "I am not my particles; besides, they are all renewed every seven years. I believe that, in death, I will not lose my humanity; it will be enlarged and more truly what it is." The universe expands. I wonder: is there ever an ultimate draft, the project finished, God brushing His palms together with a hardy feeling of satisfaction? Which draft am I?

Today, popular music is filled with obscenities unthinkable during the period Rodgers and Hart were composing. Dancing too has taken many forms, from the ceremonial movements of Egyptian priests, Romans, and Greeks, to the mating rituals of Aztecs, to Italian Renaissance ballet, the waltzes of the mid-eighteen-hundreds so adored by Queen Victoria, to tangos and rumbas, modern dance, old school slams, and the totally unvarnished display of twerking. There may be a metaphorical relationship between sexual and spiritual desire. They each contain that innate longing for completion, as in the Persian poetry of Rumi and Kabir. But with the explicit performances of Miley Cyrus, Nicki Minaj, and others, there's no attempt at metaphor. It's just sex.

It's also possible that one day, music will be imbedded in our brain. All we'll have to do is think "Dancing on the Ceiling," and hark, the violins. But how will our memory keep up? So many songs composed every year, so many albums and concerts. Sound waves splice through the air; radiate out, finally crashing against the shore of distant planets and stars. The cosmic beach is littered with songs, and only some are strong enough to return.

On our mantel sits a little brown box bearing one fifth of my mother's ashes. Thus far, there has been no scattering. She died decades ago and yet, for me, she lives on—in the cashmere sweater I inherited, in her annotated poetry books, and most of all, in my dreams. There, my mother flees, not to heaven, but to a rented apartment on P Street in Georgetown, just blocks away from where I grew up. She never answers the phone. Groceries are delivered, but her mail is held indefinitely by the post office. I've complained in my sleep (says my husband): "Mom, can you please tell me where you are?" Her retreat is painful to everyone she knew, particularly her five daughters. This is the posthumous existence she's chosen, these phantasms planted in my subconscious, where I am helpless, and she is free of responsibility and obligation. And yet, I do not blame her one bit.

Jessie Matthews is dead. Rodgers and Hart are dead. Jeri Southern worked in Chicago clubs and became known for her torch songs and even made the top ten song list. But she suffered with paralyzing performing anxiety and depression, and was rumored to be an alcoholic and diabetic, although the cause of death was a heart attack. Perhaps "Dancing on the Ceiling" has staying power because so many singers have covered it. Popularity is certainly one clue to music's lasting value. There must be some quality driving that continuing popularity—excellence, beauty, and a message that instantly connects to an audience. "Dancing on the Ceiling" contains all this, in spades.

This woman is lying sleepless, nestled under a bedspread. Her lover may be practicing a waltz in the apartment above, his footsteps following diagrams on the floor, waiting for just the right moment to invite her to the ball. We'll never know for sure. The woman locked in the song is a stargazer. She sleeps alone. But now he approaches, whispers in her ear. His breath is cinnamon-scented. She can almost sense his palm against her back, its confidence and heat. The folds of her chiffon skirt brush against her calves. He dips her silently and...Lo, the chandelier with its tiny bulbs like champagne bubbles.

Is this it, the promised land? A splash of light to lure her away from family and friends? A puff of breath from the mouth of God to speed her along to heaven? This is what we do when the facts are just out of reach—we *suppose*.

"Hyfrydol,"
Composer: Rowland H. Prichard (1830)

Lewes is a small town in coastal Delaware, population roughly three thousand, except during the summer, when it swells by at least twice that number of people. Its motto is "First town in the first state." In 1986, this is where my nascent family of four landed with no job prospects, no plans, only a longing to live some place other than the mobbed New York environs. My father offered an upstairs apartment in his early 1900s house on Market Street. The rent was $150 a month, a good thing since our only source of income was a bi-monthly check from the Office of Unemployment. Jeffrey picked up an adjunct teaching position in nearby Salisbury, but otherwise our only tasks were attending to our children, applying for jobs, and writing. My father's mother Fay took a turn in a third apartment but fled back to New York City within months. Too close to the morgue, she said.

The town was virtually abandoned in the winter. We were strangers, overwhelmed by our squabbling daughters, and eager to get out of the house. Any house of worship would do on our very first Sunday. With the girls in tow, we descended our narrow, stairway with its pipe railing, picked our way down the slushy driveway, and once on Market Street, turned left. A few blocks away, we noticed a group of parishioners filing into a Thomas Hardy vision: a steepled brick sanctuary with the requisite stained glass and small graveyard beside. We entered and sat down at the rear. Moments later we noticed the blue welcome card where clearly was written "St. Paul's Episcopal Church." Okay. We'd give it a whirl.

The priest was young, small in stature, and married to a very tall woman with two kids. The liturgy moved along quickly. His sermon referenced the ocean (it was very close by). We stood and sang the first hymn, number 426, "Hyfrydol" or "Love Divine, All Loves Excelling." The priest's favorite and, a few services later, mine too. I was hooked. The hymns, especially this one, were my way in. Over the next year or so, I came for the music, the singing, and the sweet little choir's harmonics.

There are those who see this as a sin or, at best, a distraction—an off-the-mark path to the religious life. C.S. Lewis chastised his parishioners, "If God…wanted music, He would not tell *us*. For all our offerings whether of music or martyrdom, are like the intrinsically worthless present of a child, which a father values indeed, but values only for the intention." Fortunately, he came about, granting that music could complicate and deepen the language in a service. "But as I went on, I realized that the hymns were, nevertheless, being sung with devotion and benefit by an old saint in elastic-side boots in the opposite pew, and then you realize that you aren't fit to clean those boots. It gets you out of your solitary conceit." Church music had value; it just wasn't crucial in the journey towards God. But it helped, at least in my case. In time, other parts of the liturgy filtered into my consciousness too, whether accompanied by a choir or not. There was the call and response There was the call and response (*Lord have mercy upon us, Christ have mercy upon us*), The Nicene Creed, the Prayers of the People (where I could speak aloud the names of loved ones lost or suffering), The Confession, The Peace, The Great Thanksgiving, The Breaking of the Bread, and The Lord's Prayer. All the comfortable words.

First published in 1549, the *Book of Common Prayer* derives from the plainsong of the Roman Gradual for the Mass. On close inspection you can see that some of it is written in iambic pentameter, which we know occurs in poetry, plays, and song. I took to the King James translation. The elevated language seemed right for the occasions of prayer, communion, and gratitude. To me, the contemporary versions—"you" and "your" instead of "thy" and "thine,"—blur the line between holy and everyday speech, like serving a fancy dinner on paper plates. Of course, there are plenty of folks who are comfortable with a more contemporary parlance.

There is a reason the King James liturgy is notorious for its beauty. The utterances and phrases are exquisitely balanced, dense with meaning yet graceful in diction. I could follow the rhythm, immerse myself in each compact expression. *Thy kingdom come; thy will be done on earth as it is in heaven.* Here is the core of a belief in God, laid out like musical intervals—here and there, self and other, minor and major. The symmetry was consoling. Someone else was in charge and this Someone was every-where. There was *Give us this day our daily bread*, which anchored me to the present and arrived in the form of bread, that most basic of foods. Then, *forgive us our trespasses as we forgive those who trespass against us*, like an octave struck on a piano with thumb and pinky, one note collaborating with the other to double or deepen the sound and purpose. Half of the expression was useless without the other.

The Welsh word "*Hyfrydol*," pronounced *hevredull*, means "cheerful." If you are in the right place at the right time, the song brims with optimism, and no wonder. Its full melody (excepting one note) is constructed of just five notes of a major scale. This alone creates something that virtually anyone can sing. The melody's contours repeated or traveling in multiple directions—up, down, with rests and pauses—display an elegance that's hard to resist. And the meter sits well. If you scan the text and translate this to numbers, there are two patterns, one with eight syllables (Love-di-vine-all-loves-ex-cel-ling) and another with seven (Joy-of-heav'n-to-earth-come-down). This recurs four times, encouraging even a stiff, devotional body to rock.

My engagement with the song was more than a little sentimental. It could easily have been the score for the Lewes, Delaware, chapter of our lives. We were experiencing an unusual reprieve from two mind-numbing, poor-paying jobs: my husband manager of a small security company, and me a free-lance writer for a local bank. Both of us hired to aggressively peddle, whether our product was guard services or the benefits of banking with the now-defunct City Trust Bank. Oh, we were grateful all right, especially for the natural bonuses: time to read deeply, salty offshore breezes, exploring the so-called DelMarVa peninsula with our young daughters, bluefish, and crab right off the boat.

In *Swann's Way*, in the midst of his meditations on memory, Proust wrote: "I feel that there is much to be said for the Celtic belief that the souls of those whom we have lost are held captive in some inferior being, in an animal, in a plant, in some inanimate object."

They also believed in a life after death and, like many cultures they buried food, weapons, and ornaments with the dead. One year, on our way up to Door County, Wisconsin, I drove to the cemetery where I paced the grounds until I found my mother's marker, a small brass container buried up to its neck with a screw-on cap. Clearly meant for flowers. Instead, I placed photographs inside—of my two girls. While my family waited in the car, I said a prayer, twice, then returned to the car, and never came back.

Why is the idea of God so stubbornly planted in our consciousness? Why the deep, uncanny longing so prevalent among humans, the *sehnsucht, Hiraith, soudade, senardá, morrina, dor, cianalas, tizita, toska, duende,* that leaves us pining for something beyond the earthly claptrap of our brains. We may be connected to families and friends; still, we strongly suspect we're exiles in the universe, longing for home, and transformation. We admit we don't know what happens after death. Or we just believe. Or there's nothing, said my father, the nihilist. Either way we are caught up in mystery and a dilemma. As Pascal wrote in his *Wager,* "We see too much to deny and too little to be sure." And, in his book, *How to Be,* the Gethsemane monk Paul Quenon imagines death as an entrance into the totality of everything. The afterlife is "a fractal—a complex never-ending pattern." But to gain totality, we must stop asking, *What's in it for me? It's* fruitless to speculate. Who knows what lies in store for us if anything? So, if you think a song like a child's queer hum is a one-off, dead upon arrival, think again. Some father or mother may remember it. Someone with talent and musical inclinations may place it at the center of a score. There are many examples of musical reinvention in "*Hyfrydol.*" Consider the various lyrics, its translation of "*Hyfrydol*" into multiple languages, the arrangement and settings tailor-made for each instrument—organ, brass, timpani, and all levels of voice. I believe music can lead us to believe. I was a late bloomer, a perennial, sleeping the winter away under sand, clay, and rock. I woke to a hymn written almost two hundred years ago by an adolescent loom tender's assistant, and lyrics by the manager of a maritime insurance company. Who would have suspected? Who could have known?

*

Deep down, she's always felt ten years younger than her actual age, whatever her age. So, it came as a surprise to hear how seriously her brain had declined. There were changes in her behavior: loss of focus while driving, forgetting names and words, trouble keeping up with her younger colleagues and friends; they spoke so rapidly. Difficulty formulating sentences verbally, confusion while seated at her laptop, inability to keep up with technology, misplacing her phone, etc. She had to admit she'd forgotten to turn off the burner on the stove once or twice. For a second or two, on her drive downtown, she swerved over the double line, not recognizing any landmarks, or where she was. Once, her daughter, with a daughter in the backseat, screamed MOM.

She made an appointment to see a psychologist, who administered various cognitive tests: a long series of questions, definitions of words (which she aced), a rapid fire of X's and Y's across a white screen to measure her reaction time, then *spell these words backwards, move these blocks into the pictured pattern, add this number to this set of numbers.* It was supposed to last six hours, but at four, she called it quits. The psychologist was only measuring her fatigue. After a break for a visit to the restroom, he told her this story: a man brings his family to a pizza restaurant, where they celebrate his daughter's birthday. Suddenly, the girl begins throwing spaghetti against the wall. The manager appears in a fury and asks the parents to leave at once.

The psychologist asked her to repeat it. She complied. *Good.* The psychologist then pulled out another test in which he asked her to remember these numbers: 8, 3, 6, 2, 5, 9, 1, 4, 7. Now, remember these words: moss, Poland, character, noodle, satisfy, Toyota, Spain, situation, beach, hairbrush, tomato, bridge. *Repeat as many as you can.* She managed about half. She was doing so well on the word definitions and only missed one! The psychologist then said, *now tell me the story again.*

A mere week later, the results of the tests were in. The psychologist sat down behind his desk, drew his hands apart, demonstrating this: *Here are the two poles: white and black. Your cognitive level hovers around dark gray. It is not Alzheimer's, nor dementia (just yet). But there are changes in your behavior. I am advising you to do as little driving as possible, carry a notebook in your purse so you can write down reminders. In your purse, you should keep your reading glasses, wallet, and phone, as well. Carry your purse wherever you go.*

She handled it all reasonably well, said the psychologist to her husband and two daughters. This was the only positive comment the psychologist made. What sort of music should accompany *this* experience? "Fur Elise" on her father's harpsichord where many of the plectrum are now rotten? An annoying malfunction in Cecelia's microphone? A live concerto performance where the clarinetist stopped suddenly and blew out the spit from his mouthpiece? Books with half the chapters missing? Will the book she's writing ever be finished? Or must it be published posthumously, if at all?

"The Parting Glass,"
Wailin' Jennys

Oh, all the money that e'er I spent
I spent it in good company,
And all the harm I've e'er done
Alas it was to none but me
And all I've done for want of wit
To mem'ry now I can't recall
So, fill to me the parting glass
Good night and joy be to you all

Of all the comrades that e'er I had
I'm sorry for my going away
And all the sweethearts that e'er I've had
Would wish me one more day to stay
But since it falls unto my lot
That I should rise and you should not
I'll gently rise and I'll softly call
Good night and joy be to you all
Good night and joy be to you all

The Wailin' Jennys sing in precise synchronization, as if they are one person, a throat singer who has discovered the secret of three, not just two harmonic lines. Perhaps they *are* one person. You cannot discern a single lurch in timing, a lone offkey-note, or botched entrance.

The intro is frank, straightforward, "Oh all the money that e'er I spent..." (nothing else to do but stand before us, arms dangling, palms up and open.) "I spent it in good company..." (Guilty, yes, but there's a reasonable excuse meant to balance the spendthrift.) Then the Jennys ever so discreetly downshift their voices. It's a sweet chord they land on. It signals some reassurance and acceptance. So be it. The end is nigh.

Sometimes their words close with a snap, SpenT, wiT, loT, noT, nighT, and we are reminded of the inevitable cut off facing the departing one. But these too are offset with the softer consonants of "fall," "all," "call," and "away." Both insist the time is brief for apologies, confessions, and pleas for forgiveness. We must get on with it. The Jennys stretch out the "I" till it rings like "ayeee," which could be brogue or an anxious "here I go into the deep unknown..."

The refrain is a toast, "Good night and joy be with you all." You imagine the scene: no castle or stately dining hall, but a pub in rural Scotland abutting a fog-dampened road. The floor shivers and gives, the chairs scrape, a large oak table is pocked and stained with spills and imprints of cigarette butts. It's intimate and sad—family and friends now standing and drawing close, acknowledging the arrival of a final send-off, lifting their glasses of port or sherry or whisky, whatever their taste.

And yet, it's not quite their time to rise. Thank God for that. We imagine a few quiet "Hear! Hears!" And slowly the mourners back away, open the door, depart. Now the Jennys repeat their refrain, "Good night and joy be with you all." They pause and assemble their last chord, a diminished triad, a stack of minor thirds. The sound is destabilizing, adding an air of tension, as it must be for any transition to take place. "Good night and joy be with you all."

A song is a living thing that occupies a body very briefly. Either it dies from lack of use, or it moves along through the centuries evolving, as generations come and go. Specific occasions contribute to its endurance. Consider the lullaby, the birthday, the prayer, holidays, and patriotic songs. Publication helps too. Some say "The Parting Glass" belongs to the Scots because it was included in the Skene Manuscript (*Ancient Scotish (sic) Melodies*), a collection of eighty-five airs published in the mid-1600s, produced for (or by, it's uncertain) John Skene of Halyards Castle, Lothian.

But the lyrics go back even earlier to the early 1600s when the first verse showed up in a letter by a Border Reiver named Armstrong on the occasion of his execution for the murder of Sir John Carmichael, of Edrom. *That* became a poem called "Armstrong's Goodnight," occasionally attributed to "Anonymous:"

This night is my departing night,
For here nae langer I stay;
There's neither friend nor foe o' mine
But wishes me away.

When we are scorned, judged, jailed, and executed, anonymous is what we must become.

The music itself is a little harder to trace. The lyrics have been linked to a fiddle tune known as "The Peacock," thanks to their inclusion in James Aird's *Selection of Scots, English, Irish, and Foreign Airs* in 1782. No doubt it goes further back than that. It is common for traditional musicians to borrow and steal both lyrics and melodies. Enter Robert Burns in 1788 with his phenomenally popular "Auld Lang Syne." Did he swipe a verse or two from the hapless Reiver? Perhaps. In any case, "The Parting Glass" couldn't keep up and quickly fell from grace, at least among the Scots. In came the Irish, who picked up the slack, performing and reworking it to such a degree they "rightfully" claimed it as their own. Today, there is still dispute, the words over generations inflected by dialect and mispronunciation till they acquired entirely unique and unintended meanings. It's difficult to locate a definitive version, but that, I think, is what makes it interesting, as if "The Parting Glass" were its own being, a time traveler, or a Zelig, absorbing and rejecting fragments of the various eras it passes through.

There's an overpowering scent in the pub, emanating from quarter-size splashes and rivers of Guinness on the bar and sticky indoor/outdoor carpet. The guests are liquored up, their tongues, breath, and conversation producing in the air a second scrim of booze. The men bump shoulders and rub the sparse hair on the poor soul's head. Women young and old cover him with sloppy kisses. Here and there an argument breaks out. It's *de rigueur*—one expects a disagreement when you blend Scot and Irish, and a lot of drinking. After all, they're Celts, notorious quibblers with the same hot blood. We might even call them cousins, famous for their courage, stubbornness, fire, and wit. "All their wars are merry, and all their songs are sad," said Chesterton.

Here come the fiddles, bagpipes, and whistles too. I read somewhere: "Irish music is like a well-rounded smooth river rock, while Scottish music is more like a jagged piece of granite that fell off of a rock face." But not tonight.

In the moment of "The Parting Song," the departing one accepts fate and blithely dismisses trivial details, wrongs inflicted, mistakes made, and petty insults suffered. He has reached an understanding and stands within the Celtic in-between, one foot among the living, and the other hovering above an unknown land. The stricken and condemned have settled, a mature example to the living friends and family standing about. Together they all begin to relax, cradle their mugs and glasses and cups, with drink and forgiveness all around.

And what shall be our parting glass? Crystal, tin, china, silver, or gold? A "kapala" fashioned from the skull of a monastery's founder? We too want a talisman that signals farewell, sweeter and more lasting than a train whistle or horn. The urge to leave something behind, some mark on the world is extremely powerful. We've produced music, paintings, poetry, architecture, and countless other art forms with the unspoken wish to be remembered. In the act of making, we seem to say, "Here is a thing of beauty, made more beautiful because crafted by me, a single being unlike any other being."

I rummage through my storage boxes and find a salt-fired ceramic goblet—the only piece of pottery remaining from my apprenticeship decades ago. It wasn't purchased or stolen or passed down from someone else. I remember wedging the grog-speckled, clammy earth into a pyramid, slapping it on the wheel, and leaning rigid into the spinning clay till I had it centered. Then the cavity formed with both thumbs, the walls drawn upward, thinned, the lip flattened with an elephant ear sponge. Next the base, shaped like a miniature nuclear tower. Both cut from the wheel with a wire and left to stiffen overnight, then tooled and trimmed and joined at the waist, one on top of the other with a little slip and crosshatching to secure the coupling. The sponge again, dipped in water to smooth the joinery, flatten petty nicks and bumps till they slowly disappear. Then brushed with under-glaze, fired to cone ten in a salt kiln, and left to rest overnight. Finally, the great reveal—so pleasurable to potters—the bricks removed, the goblet with its sheen and random imperfections (salt pools and dark spots called "angel kisses.") Then carefully slid out, cooled in the night air, ready to be filled. This will be *my* parting glass.

That said, I must point out the goblet—though handmade—is special only to me, a weak bid for immortality. Indeed, we think too much of things when considering our legacy. Should we make a list, a fair division of twelve beloved crystal champagne glasses? How to distribute the larger pieces, the harpsichord and 1830s Swedish baking table, cannonball bed, oak kitchen hutch with its secret drawer? Hopefully our choices will satisfy. Would it be better to draw straws? Objects have their own laws, and we have no say regardless of our investment in them. A sentimental friend might place the goblet on the mantle or store it in archival tissue and bubble wrap for posterity. More likely, there's selling, burning, gifting, losing, and smashing. I tell myself to swallow my portion of tepid wine, the most I can take away. Later my survivors will pack up my books, the diaries, and drafts. But no object can stand in for the person we love.

I have a friend named Tess, who lost her husband after just ten years of marriage. She was slow in accepting his death, or, as she put it, in getting to know the new Ray, so much quieter than the old Ray. There were social occasions of course, friends and relatives bringing their share of him to the table, joining it with the other stories, jokes, and poetry. These gifts were helpful, but they couldn't possibly make a whole Ray.

✳

The father died at ninety-three in late December 2021, his life spanning nearly twice the number of years as his wife's. Four decades from her death, the contrast still seems unjust, ill-considered by whatever being was in charge. This not-quite-buried resentment persists in those who loved and cannot forget her, the warm and too briefly present mother.

Preparations for her father's memorial service began: an online memorial webpage. The guest list and invitations. A call for donations to the Institute. Recollections gathered up by the sisters, timed for five minutes each, precisely. One colleague and two friends granted a little more time to ramble. The current president of the UI, down with COVID, promised to Zoom in a contribution. She curated a playlist with her son-in-law, who wisely featured the most familiar of the father's favorites. A simple program passed around; the text printed in blue ink.

Bach BMV208—"Sheep May Safely Graze"
Mozart K581—"Clarinet Quintet," "Larghetto"
Albinoni—"Adagio in G Minor"
"Wade in the Water," sung by Rayshun LaMarr
Mozart K618—"Ave verum Corpus"
Beethoven—"Symphony #7 Allegretto"
Eric Satie—"Gymnopédies 1"
Bach B208—"Secular Contatas"
Leonard Cohen—"Halleluiah," sung by Rayshun LaMarr

September 2022: She and her family flew into Washington, D.C., a city utterly changed since she lived there in the sixties and early seventies. Long gone were those sleepy days as kids, wandering barefoot and unsupervised through neighborhoods now dominated by condominiums, office buildings, and roads jammed with tourists and traffic. The Urban Institute itself was sporting a bright, windowed addition, with curves like a reposing swan. This, in contrast to the original building, square as a piece of Lego, its windows sunken into neo-brutal cement.

The new interior included state-of-the-art technology, views of the Washington Monument, Jefferson Memorial, the National Cathedral, and the shining but distant Potomac. The service took place in the auditorium where sound seemed chiseled, a cool sharp knife through white paper. Chairs were arranged in a half-moon, the seats covered with padded leather. One wall was occupied by an enormous screen displaying super-sized, black-and-white photographs of her father the Eagle Scout, the thirty-something whiz kid striding off an anchored battleship, all smiles. And his doting mother Fay (both blonde). There were photos with JFK and LBJ. Some included his family, the daughters dressed in neon-colored horizontal stripes, their mother wearing a Jackie Kennedy shift and jacket. It was that time. Together they made an impeccable vision of a happy family. These were the sixties; parental roles were clearly defined and mostly accepted. Women stayed at home; men worked late. The father traveled often, raising money for his nonprofit. For the most part he was married to his job. But on occasion—and greatly appreciated—his children were granted a bit of his individual attention.

After their mother passed away, the four sisters quickly married—the men were solid, realistic, and talented. Amazingly, they are still married today. There followed seven grandchildren, and six great-grandchildren, many of whom the father never knew, except in photographs. In one picture, five of the great-grandchildren form a pyramid, a teetering jumble of skinny arms and legs, the littlest (with the biggest head) on top.

There was a green room, where the sisters practiced their brief eulogies. Roughly three hundred and fifty guests were in attendance, on Zoom and in person. It was sobering—the signs of aging, the heavy mascara, the stooped posture and loss of height, paper-thin skin on a friend's hand. Some mourners were unrecognizable, until they shared their names.

There was a point when she stood alone, confused, her ankle and right shoulder throbbing, despite comfortable clothes and low heels. She tried to follow conversations but speaking at length to one person meant ignoring the others. It was overwhelming and she soon abandoned the idea of catching up with her extended family, unseen for a decade or more. Thankfully, the guests moved outside, where she spotted the youngest and eldest of the grandchildren, devouring pizza and tiny crustless sandwiches, bonding beautifully amid rushing waiters and musicians.

Alas, the music she and her son-in-law had carefully curated, sifting through dozens of possibilities—their choices—tempo, conductor, and singer; all were reduced to a distant knell from aloft. The songs were barely decipherable. Before the room filled up, she was able to discern the tail end of Albinoni's "Adagio." But real star of show was the singer Rayshun LaMarr, who opened with "Wade in the Water," in person, *a cappella*. With his shiny pate, sculpted black beard, and intense stare, no one would have argued for another choice. The man had incredible range and could have cast his voice through several more tiers of seated listeners. And yet, it was an intimate, heartfelt performance, his face sweeping the audience and drawing it in.

Tributes and narratives flew by without incident and rarely a cough or mispronunciation. There were admiring recollections of the father, his many accomplishments in both the Kennedy and Johnson administrations. He was considered a giant in public policy. A man who, among other things, gave Robert McNamara a carefully worked out review of the costs and benefits of an all-volunteer army, taking into account both financial and human terms. He used the best of the analytic tools he learned at Stanford and the Rand Corporation, adding to them his own common sense, intelligence, and compassion.

There were nods from his daughters too. In the early sixties he arranged for one sister's adoption from a Korean orphanage, a life changer for the four-year-old little girl. He shelled out college tuitions for all four girls. And who could forget the tenderness he displayed towards his profoundly disabled daughter, the youngest who died in a nursing home at the age of forty-one. At her birth, he'd opposed keeping her at home. Then, after their mother passed away, he took complete responsibility, visited weekly, played with his child's lush curly hair (for she was eternally a child), massaged her shoulders, and stroked her hands. He also figured out a way to bring music to her, including the liveliest spirituals and, of course, Beethoven. She loved the drama and clapped her hands vigorously. There were generosities indeed.

LaMarr closed the service with a buoyant cover of Leonard Cohen's "Hallelujah," substituting that singer's unremitting drone with joyous high notes, spreading his fingers and arms wide and inviting all to join the chorus. Her father would have loved it.

The mourners then took elevators to a roof deck that jutted out into the sky, bedecked with flowers, and flapping red and white umbrellas, a live jazz band, a scurry of elegantly jacketed servers with plates of lamb-pops, cheeses, miniature hamburgers, gourmet pizzas, and most popular of all, an array of oysters on a long table and three kinds of hot sauce.

Her father's bicycle, the one he built from European parts, the one he rode to work and home along the C&O canal's towpath, was polished up and displayed in front of the elevator doors. He would have loved that too.

*

Mortality is a very thin slice of adulthood, the body trucking its way to the ash heap, increasingly accompanied by imperfect balance, dimming eyes, an array of pills to take, voice thinning to a wheeze, a reed without its clarinet. It's thin everything: bone, hair, worn-out clothing, time. And, if we live to a hundred, we are not necessarily blessed. Speech is boiled down to one or two phrases. Then a head nod for yes, shake for no. The mouth drained of saliva, tongue the texture of twigs. At the end, it was reduced to her father's noiseless thumbs up, away wave for leave me alone. Don't worry about paying for the home (said those in charge), the end comes quickly, at best (worst?) two years. The father landed the many windowed "corner office" of his nursing home where he sat motionless before a well-manicured landscape of trees and parked cars. His daughter could not guess what he'd been thinking, or, more ominously, what the absence of thought might feel like. At some point he shuffled towards the bed, lay down, and with a sigh, entered eternity.

In contrast, the mother died at home in her ages-old four-poster bed. She'd had enough of hospitals and preferred to go out, her way. First, she resisted food, then water. More than anything else, she wanted to spare her children. Her memorial service took place in the backyard. A small gathering of friends and family stood sweating in the heat and humidity surrounded by yellow daisies and forsythia. The sisters shared their reflections: how she memorized Frost's poetry while driving a VW van up the Atlantic coast. How smart their mother was, how tuned to her kids. How she loved to have her hair played with too, and the daughters submitted. She was a housewife who earned a master's degree in literature from Stanford, studying with Ivor Winters and writing her master's thesis on Melville's *Billy Budd*. She was assuredly not the esteemed public figure her husband was. Instead, she was a practical person who understood that the city of Washington had few options for a disabled child like hers. She took up the cause in both public and private, publishing one of the first directories filled with resources for handicapped children. It was a modest portion of fame but an extremely important one for the movement away from institutionalization.

And yet, lying in her bed, propped up with two enormous pillows, she wondered aloud if she had contributed anything to their lives. Oh yes, the sisters assured her. She was the parent who knew each of her children individually and thoroughly. By her model, they knew how to love, even when it wasn't easy. The mother then dictated a handful of notes to relatives and friends, along with a few recipes she knew the girls loved: her spaghetti sauce, Korean beef, spareribs, Spanish rice, chicken pot pie, beef tenderloin (special occasions only, don't mind the cost!).

They endure to this day. Her pecan puff cookies and orange tortes were passed around the table for generations. On holidays in the kitchen, she basted the turkey, whipped up the mashed potatoes, seasoned the green beans, and added pecans, cranberries, apples, and raisins to the stuffing. She cooked with elan and a sense of humor. One year, she strode into the dining room with the heavily laden platter, misstepped, and watched the bird slide to the floor. She headed back to the kitchen, picked off the dirt, returned to the table, and lightly announced, "Thank goodness I have this back-up turkey." In a pinch, she could work wonders.

"King and Lionheart,"
Vocals: Of Monsters and Men

"Howling ghosts they reappear
In mountains that are stacked with fear
But you're a king and I'm a lionheart
A lionheart..."

—Nanna Bryndis Hilmarsdottir

Forward.

The song is set on repeat. The infant, though scarcely a foot long, shifts inside its mother, resembling a mouse under a carpet or small mogul. The mother's skin accommodates, for the nudge reassures despite its inconvenient timing, far into the night when she would be sleeping. Everyone else is sleeping, but this does not make her feel isolated or lonely. After all, she's not one, but two beings, each with a heart, a brain, and two lungs. From a paper cup on the tray, she takes a sip of Sprite. A wonder, how this clear, nutrition-free liquid will turn to milk. But not yet.

Back.

The contractions begin early and real. Not unusual for a woman with three previous pregnancies and strong Braxton-Hicks—but worth an ultrasound at the hospital, half an hour away. The examination room too cold, the frigid gel shocking her belly, the probe shaped like one of her pink rubber erasers from elementary school. Kind of a miracle how sound and echoes are transformed to data then image, a printed copy of which the parents can take home with them. Their baby wobbles around on the black and white monitor like a lava light. At which point they discover it's a boy, quiet electricity circulating the room (all the other children are girls).

However, there's no time for celebration. The tech excuses herself and a specialist steps in to report there's suspicious fluid around the baby's heart, in the abdominal cavity, and more in the shape of a dark sickle moon above his head. It's called Hydrops, an "edema in at least two fetal compartments," though it might be the name of a Greek demon too. Will the monster drown the little king?

After three Fetal Maternal Medicine doctors weigh in, it becomes apparent they really aren't sure what is happening here. One concludes the anatomical survey was essentially normal and the baby just has a virus; another says it's a chromosomal disorder with a 50/50 chance of live birth—a huge range, leading the father to hunt down likely etiologies online. To some, this might seem unwise, but considering the prospect of death or lifetime care of a disabled son, medical research might serve as a distraction, or mourning, or even a balm.

The song blasts from an SUV's cheap speakers. The grandmother dislikes it at first and says so. What it does for the mother she doesn't understand. The band is from Iceland and, true, she longs to wander through those stark landscapes and seaside villages with their brightly painted dwellings. But the lead singer Nanna opens with a popcorn soprano: "Taking over this town, they should worry…" each syllable pricking the air. Her accent is heavy too and the only line the grandmother can decipher is: "That we won't run, we won't run, we won't run…" Three chances to capture three words.

Forward.

Several days later, the mother is again called in. With held breath she's monitored, poked, and scanned. And yet, there's good news: the fluid level appears to have stabilized. So, let's do this outpatient, says the doc. "Cautiously optimistic," she's sent home. At the next examination, his optimism is confirmed; the fluid is reabsorbed—an excellent outcome. The whole family exhales.

Back.

Prone on the couch, the mother rips out her ear buds and the song retreats to a metallic squeak no one can read. She has to be sure. How long since the little one stirred? It feels like ages. Even when she presses deep into her belly, she feels nothing: no flutter or primordial roll of the baby's shoulder. And this was an active kid. There's plenty of room to flip and kick, so the lack of movement is worrisome. The father borrows a home Doppler kit. A normal fetal heartbeat at thirty-three weeks averages 120-160 bpm. The machine reads over three hundred. He checks again; can't be right. Maybe the Doppler is broken and picked up the mother's heartbeat too. They wait for the appointment the next morning. Again, older kids stashed with the grandparents. Suitcase packed just in case. The same chilly examination room, monitor, and icy gel, the tech waving her wand back and forth setting in motion that ultrasound magic. After two or three minutes she cuts short her pleasant chatter, exits into the hall to alert the resident physician. The Doppler was correct; his heart is beating at least twice the normal rate. The baby's in Supra Ventricular Tachycardia, or SVT. That word—*tachycardia*—could be a monster or a dangerously swift dinosaur.

What follows is a stream of specialists. For the mother and son—high-risk FMM doctors in addition to her regular OB/GYN. For the infant—Neonatologist, Pediatric Cardiologist, Neurologist, Cardiac Electrophysiologist. A quick decision to force the birth, to cut and lift the infant out of the mother's abdomen like a leg of lamb.

What does the infant see, if anything, when the shell cracks open and light blares? What does it feel like when the heart's in SVT? The baby cannot speak, though adults with the syndrome have described a palpable flop or hiccough to start things off then suddenly the race is on, accompanied by vertigo, weakness, neck pulsations, and sweating. It's been compared to a sustained panic attack and the mother can tell you about that: a tidal wave of fear, elevated pulse rate, hyperventilation, usually resolved by breathing into a paper bag. Better yet—husband, grandmother, or sister to hold her, to make real that species-wide sensation of safety in enclosure.

Again, she screws in her ear buds—counterclockwise—securing a seal, muting the buzzers, bells, and visitor voices. "King and Lionheart," from the album *My Head Is an Animal,* carries her back to the ordinary expectations of pregnancy: steady growth, healthy pulse, and assurance of a normal birth. It's the only music she can listen to continually, the rhythm and voice and strum in direct contrast to her son's out-of-sync beat. If this were a fairytale, the lyrics might be sorcery, stabilizing his heart, making everything all right. "We're here to stay, we're here to stay, we're here to stay."

There's a light knock. The FMM surgeon slides in. On his first visit, he wore street clothes, thick black rimmed glasses, and a wavy '70s haircut. His shoulders are hunched, frame rather slight. Not reassuring at first glance. Now he's Superman, upright in scrubs, muscles bulging in his sleeves, gold cross on a chain to summon his god and banish those demons. He's the perfect candidate to rescue a preemie in distress then fly off into the sunset after a long, gory battle won single-handedly. They look up his profile and, sure enough, Superman did his fellowship and residency on a San Diego naval base. He was in the military. Okay then.

On the gurney, she feels a little kick and asks, hopefully, is a C-section really necessary at this point? Without comment, the surgical nurse slips a hairnet over her patient's long hennaed hair and surrounds her with paper sheets in preparation for the epidural. She scolds, she scolds, *Oh, it's not that bad, now, is it?*

Stupid woman, it's not the needle making her cry; it's the baby. Fortunately, a second nurse nudges the mean one aside and wordlessly cradles the patient between her enormous breasts.

And what is the family thinking, confined to a cramped waiting room, the magazines untouched, the television on mute? Oh, it's just another Cesarean, her third. Needn't worry. But the grandmother was present for the other births and this time his status is high risk and she's ousted from the delivery room. No one is talking much, and she can't sit still, so she hunts down a Dr Pepper, her daughter's soda of choice. Down the elevator to the lobby and the gift store is locked. At ten am on a Monday? What if there's news and the doctor is there and now, she's missing it. Up the elevator to the second floor through an endless corridor with its clever sign showing the precise number of footsteps to the cafeteria. But will he be okay, will he crawl, stand, cruise, walk, even run. At the base of the escalator are three vending machines with Cokes and Sprites and Dasani water, nothing else. Oh please. Need to get back. Taking too long. She fills a cup with ice at the fountain but the tab for Dr Pepper is broken. And the baby could be stillborn, and the family would be broken. And the muffins look terrible and the shampoo her daughter requested is out of stock in the hospital's gift shop. Now she remembers, and the worst part of the song cycles through her head: "Howling ghosts they reappear/In mountains that are stacked with fear…" She tries to shrug it off—he's no ghost; he's not even born yet.

At least there are three other children. Some physicians have a script, their communication so practiced it feels both weightless and consequential, like screen doors you swing out of the way before putting a hand on the door. But this FMM physician is vibrating in her wrinkled white coat. *Your baby is very sick. We don't know what's wrong with him.* What she did not say: the child coded once for forty-five seconds. As the mother's recovery room is in the adjacent hospital, accessible by an enclosed glass walkway, she's unaware of at least two heroic efforts to revive him. The gray-blue skin and rapid chest compressions because paddles will not do. Two IV lines, one for the "big gun" medicine Atropene, the other simple saline injected simultaneously, speeding the drug to his heart. Watch it on a monitor, flat line cresting on the ECG like a shard of glass.

The baby is a long way from deep chest laughing; from the breast milk bond and dopamine that relaxes both mother and child; a long way from sashaying in his father's arms, back and forth, round and round. He's tucked into the apparatus—a clear plastic bin sterilized just that morning. A cloth over his eyes is folded and anchored by tape to a horseshoe pillow securing his head. He wears a vest of wires and pads strapped to his chest like a suicide bomb. The bag of fluid is nothing like lactation and a needle and tube are poor stand-ins for the nipple.

The father's heard the near-death story, but wisely holds it back. The mother will not know the details for weeks. No one mentions the buzzers and urgency, the scuffle of nurses and physicians, their own pulses rising as the infant twists and jerks. She'll be grateful for the ignorance, even if it's ignorance without bliss.

The best way to cradle an infant is skin to skin. Rocking imitates the motion of amniotic fluid. It's common knowledge that a lullaby coaxes a baby to sleep, slowing the child's heartbeat and breath. These songs are generally simple and repetitive, with a 6/8 beat—a nice balance of boring and just interesting enough to capture the child's attention. NICU studies show that preemies exhibit less stress during IV sessions when music is played and, over time, they gain more weight. Adults can be similarly bewitched by a smooth-coated voice, or a spoon stirring in a teacup. A hypnotist will swing a watch back and forth till the patient is under. Even animals will go there, needing little to induce a trance. A basset hound slinks in slow motion under a Christmas tree, ornaments lightly grazing its back, and other dogs brush against tablecloths, hung laundry, or houseplants. It's called "ghost-walking," or simply, "trancing."

Hospitals now offer a variety of nonstandard therapies, including massage, increased attention to diet, and engagement with art. In Louisville, there's music therapist Brian Schreck, who pioneered a treatment for terminal patients and their families, calling it "Sounds of Life," though the medical names—heartbeat intervention, or music therapy cardiography—are more precise. Schreck is no amateur. He studied music at Berklee College of Music and New York University. Mostly, he works in the NICU, PICU, and CICU, recording the patient's heartbeat and then composing a song on his guitar that follows its rhythm. The whole family participates as he revises and polishes, moving towards a kind of survivor's lullaby, one they can return to repeatedly after the loved one has passed away. The songs are stirring, the cadence warm and insistent, as if we'd put an ear to the patient's chest. It makes me wonder why no one has thought of this before.

But "terminal" is not an acceptable word for this mother. Besides, she's already chosen her song. It's a pity she doesn't want to be touched, for she too could be cradled, should be. Instead, she swallows the soy vanilla latte, savors the oatmeal her husband brought from Starbucks—her made-to-order comfort food. A hypnotist will speak in a soft, authoritative voice and this is what the mother hears as she listens to her song: "And in the winter night sky ships are sailing,/Looking down on these bright blue city lights.../We're here to stay." She is momentarily mesmerized, carried away from the medicinal scents and surrounding apparatus and fear of mortality. A dense fog moves into her brain as...

At last, there's a diagnosis: Wolff Parkinson White syndrome, named for Louis Wolff, John Parkinson, and Paul Dudley White who mapped its electrocardiogram findings in 1930. Extra neural pathways confuse the heart, causing it to overcompensate with supra-ventricular arrhythmias, pre-excitation, and recurrent tachycardia. Milder versions have occurred in the husband's extended family. Surely the neonatal doc questioned them? Genetics is a boon for the diagnostician. For the patient, a harness held taut over generations.

Why must we confine a child to a gated bed, its rail propped at half-staff? Anxious fathers sometimes go so far as bolting its legs to the floor with metal braces. Why, when the cradle is a winged object. It swoops back and forth like a jump rope jingle: blue bells, cockleshells, Evie ivy over. Will the baby ride on his father's crossed leg, believing it's a horse? Will he sail into the sky on a swing? Will he rock the rowboat, till water gushes over its sides?

You may see him now, the doctor says. Double doors in the corridor open crossways like pinball flippers. A metal pad fastened on the wall makes them do so when tapped with an elbow. There's an unoccupied reception desk and thus, a total lack of information. The enormous trash receptacles and U-shaped curtain that sweeps aside as you enter the room. Incubators in a ring, computer-stands at twelve and six, monitors flicking like overhead train schedules, 154, 125, 89. An alarm for blood pressure and warning signal for the IV sac slumping on its pole. The vats of Purel and Hibiclens and pads and sheets and preemie-size straight-jackets. The blanket—white with pink for good health and blue for bad news? The indigo bilirubin light, glowing over his crib on the third day of his life.

At first, the mother doesn't want to see him. Seeing is bonding and he may not live. She edges in sideways, confining his image to the corner of her eye. When she finally takes it all in, she can't help thinking of *The Matrix* with its monstrous vision of birth—pods filled with liquid, fetus plugged into a far-off biological network, consciousness transferred via a dozen thick hoses, their point of contact leaving scars like inverted nipples. This baby will endure six IV sites at once. Above his incubator, a small index card recording his weight. 2.04 kilograms at birth and much of it fluid pooled in his neck, giving him a mini-Frankenstein look. She's called to nurse him for the first time, surprised that he latches on so easily. If his weight continues to rise, the baby is closer to going home. Checking will not make it rise any faster, but that index card is her touch point, better than worrying about the needles taped inside his tiny veins. One by one, they'd soon be removed, won't they?

At first, the father too is reticent and stands with his back to the incubator, following the monitors, not quite absorbing their information. They are a significant source of anxiety, but for now, easier to focus on than his son. He approaches the boy gradually, minute by minute, second by second, and then he's up close, murmuring: hello, little man, can you hear me? At this moment, the child is pink and breathing. A deeply practical man, the father sees no reason to think about the long term. The future is not palpable, contains no resolution, good or bad. And for his wife, the least he can do is force the appearance of calm. Fooling his family might metamorphose into believing it himself. Fake it till you make it.

The mother replays her anthem and shield, the music anointing her a noble beast, protector of the baby's heart. Slowly, she too evolves into a brave one, cloak around her king, atmosphere around his earth. "And as the world comes to an end/I'll be here to hold your hand/'Cause you're my king and I'm your lionheart/A lionheart."

Lullabies, like a cradle, trace an arc—both major and minor. The heart goes here and there. The lion lies down with the lamb.

The first line of defense for Wolff Parkinson White syndrome is pharmaceutical. In the NICU, Amiodarone is administered by IV drip and serves to slow and correct the baby's heart rhythm. The drug often affects thyroid function, resulting in hypo or hyperthyroidism. Synthroid is added for that too. As the days pass, the number of SVT incidents wanes and it's clear the medicine is working. The Hydrops has subsided; he's nursing well and gaining weight. The team of doctors gives the go-ahead and to everyone's great relief the baby gets to go home, discharged with a stethoscope, scripts, instructions, and the usual coupons and benign infant gear. Three older children greet their mother as she arrives, drawings and flowers and Play-Doh sculptures displayed on the kitchen table. Even the chickens are happy she's back, bustling and pooping around the front door.

The best way to hold a newborn is skin to skin, but at first, she's hesitant. The baby makes her feel like he's the first ever; she's terrified to hold him, terrified he might choke or break or suddenly code. So, the father strips off his shirt and lies down with the boy. Later, the mother orbits their bed, watching the children surround the infant, pulling on his tiny digits and poking his fuzzy cheek. Please stop, she says more than once. As much as she hated the hospital, she dearly misses its monitors and feeding tubes, the shared responsibility and beautiful black nurse who held her and wouldn't let her go. Dangerous to take him into bed, particularly at night, so she lies down next to the co-sleeper, watching the baby's chest rise and fall until it's time to feed him again.

In critical illness, there are miracles, yes. But recovery is more like an ascending/descending stock index—not without its reversals, corrections, and relapses. At home, he moves to an oral dose, administered every eight hours. Six months later, the child appears free of episodes and all medicine is off the table.

Alas, the half-life for Amio is approximately sixty days and it's precisely sixty days when his arrhythmia roars back. A full year follows, studded with relapses. They occur randomly and anywhere. Once in a bowling alley, a restaurant, the playroom of their own house. In each case, physicians are alerted in advance as mother and father sprint to the emergency room where two nurses stand by to deliver those twin silver bullets, Atropene and saline. The patient's veins are difficult to locate, and he is pricked and prodded like pie dough. Is this the best a place of healing can offer? Is this a template for the rest of the child's life? New medications in various combinations are introduced: Sotalol, Flecainide, Digoxin, a beta-blocker, Propranolol, more Amioderone, but the latter two are the only effective ones. The parents have learned to steady their panic, but coffee no longer consoles and "getting used to" is a state they never reach. Alas, "King and Lionheart" too has lost its potency. Now the lyrics remind the mother of the NICU and its abominations. Refreshing the song with a tip of her little finger doesn't make it new or effective in any way.

When her son's liver shows signs of distress, the discussion moves quickly to surgery. The baby's case is extreme. Though he's only eighteen months old and his heart very small, the doctors recommend an ablation. The technique involves mapping both healthy and accessory pathways in the heart through electrogram, performed in an electrophysiology (EP) lab. ECG monitoring electrodes are placed on the baby's chest and back. A catheter is advanced from the groin or neck using fluoroscopic guidance, rather like GPS. On the screen, the heart as a whole isn't visible, only its electrical activity, but a computer generates a ghostly simulacrum in three dimensions so surgeons can watch as the catheters snake up the torso. I've seen photos of these flexible tubes, capable of holding three separate wires, each with a tiny electrode at the tip. To me they look like lariats, designed to lasso, restrain, and kill off the offending beast. It's hard to believe a baby's veins can withstand them.

On the screen, culprit pathways look exactly as you might imagine them, flailing a bit with each heartbeat, skinny and useless like those sprouts growing between tree branches. Bad news for the tree, since they block light and draw up precious nutrients. Better to clip them carefully at the right time of the year.

And that is precisely what the surgeon does. Once the catheters are in place, he uses a radio signal generator to induce the arrhythmia, so the pathways light up, then he zaps the unhealthy tissue. This produces a scar, which cannot transmit electricity in the heart. The process is both appalling and wondrous. On a separate ECG screen, the superfluous spikes collapse, one by one. Where once there were hundreds of saw-toothed mountains, there are now ordinary hillocks and meadows.

Nervously pacing in the visitor's area, safeguarding her daughter's cell phone, the grandmother once again decides to listen to the song. It's no lullaby. What lullaby would be this quickly paced, with drumbeats and bass thudding away? She'd rather have Debussy's "Claire de Lune" or Copeland's "Saturday Night Waltz." But gradually she begins to get it, especially during the refrain—fragile and forceful, strident like a battle cry. Nanna Bryndís Hilmarsdottir was once a solo act called Songbird. Now the band is five musicians strong. Shunning the usual autobiographical stuff, their songs derive from fairy tales they tell each other. And they sing in English because it has "a lot of sharp corners." To call forth the courage in your people you must kiss the microphone, sing very loud, and brandish a lot of metal.

Today the mother sleeps more easily. She pulls her knees to her chest, tucks her head forward, hands fisted with thumbs between third and forefinger. Like a dog curling into the shell of itself, she breathes shallow for a bit, then releases out a final, long sigh. Her shoulders collapse, her mouth grows slack, hair falls over her face, but she's too far-gone to push it back. Even a Lionheart must let go once in a while.

Forward.

King Seamus wakes into his bedroom, the walls painted pale green. At three, he cannot be contained. He has mastered the art of escape no matter what his parents attempt—crib or car seat or bear hug from a father. It's not just that he's a boy; he's a crazy *fearless* boy who throws himself from precipices, who overshoots the couch and slams his substantial head against the windowsill, the bruises on either side resembling a ram's scurs. Midnight, he wanders the house, snorting over his sisters asleep in bunk beds and rousing the enormous blonde lab on the sofa. One night, he drags a barstool to the front door, climbs up the bookshelf, captures the key hidden there, opens the lock, and steps out into the moonlight. His parents try locking him into his bedroom, only to discover him the next morning, sleeping without blankets, naked on the floor. Is his desire to establish himself competing with a wish to fly apart? Which of these urges should the mother and father encourage? Will it make any difference?

Forward.

The grandmother has been entrusted with the miracle child—anointed, but just for the night. A Pack N Play is assembled beside her desk, mini-fitted sheet, lap blanket, and extra pacifier for he still suckles on one and holds the other as he sleeps. Carrying him is simple: head on shoulder, left arm the hammock and right arm the brace to keep him upright. Arms loose at his side and no argument with his sisters, who brush against him carelessly. Soon they'll be sleepy too. She treads up the stairs but it's not lassitude gripping her. This miracle is too recent, too fragile to risk any misstep. They might fall together, his bobblehead the last thing to strike the polished cement. The death of a child is an anomaly, an outrageous occurrence. She would never, ever be forgiven, least of all by herself.

What is a talisman but some object or phrase or tune or prayer you turn to for help, again and again? My daughter's favorite song held her together through a horrible crisis. After my mother died, of the many objects in her house, I chose her black cashmere sweater. A tiny Celtic gold cross is the one necklace I never take off, though I touch it constantly, especially when anxious. With each touch I pause, especially in arguments and fear. A song too, like "King and Lionheart," can be a talisman, even in the face of death. Music can be the carrier of hope: *"Howling ghosts they reappear/In mountains that are stacked with fear/But you're a king and I'm a lionheart/A lionheart."* The baby will live.

As the grandmother slides an arm under his body to position him lengthwise, the boy stirs. Could be the unfamiliar smell of the mattress, the furnace signaling on, or pure reflex. Something's not right and he breaks into a whimper, finally a revolt. Again, she eases him down with little strokes and a low register *nite, nite little king/nite, nite little king.* Though exhausted, he's still not having it. Finally, she places him on her chest and climbs into her own bed, his legs splayed off her hips, cheek to her sternum. When nursing's a faded recollection, here's one use for her breasts; he settles between hers, directly over the heart with its muscle and blood and beat. She links up their respirations, two to one, shallow, shallow, then that long exhalation. No cradle is available, so she makes the rocking sound, a tenor note that extends and drops like a foghorn off the Northeastern coast, air thick with moisture. "And in the sea, that's painted black/ Creatures lurk below the deck/But you're my king and I'm your lionheart." How sweet to mock that movement and sing that song till the boy's eyelids drop and his breath sails off on its own, and he is gloriously asleep.

*

Music retains its own language across all its forms: melodic, dissonant, formal, folk, instrumental, a cappella—in tempos from *vivace* to *largo*. It can function as a surrogate for grieving, or joy, or lust, or meditation. It can send men and women into battle with the willingness to destroy or be destroyed. It can be both background and impetus for romantic love. It can give voice to the otherwise inexpressible, in ways that written or spoken language cannot, or at best is woefully slow to match. For those in a state of despair, it offers an escape, a protected space or, at least, confirmation that suffering is shared. The best music creates a kind of holistic vibration, greater than the sum of its parts—bypassing the editor and the accountant in us all, going straight to the source of being. With its variation and repetition, predictability and surprise, music consoles, brings back the infant in us, the infant that stays with us until the end.

Acknowledgements

The author is grateful to the following literary magazines in which these essays first appeared:

Fourth Genre: "Perchoo, or The Sound of Mourning"

The Southern Humanities Review: "Be Dark Night"

The Louisville Review: "Benedictus," from Mozart's *Requiem*

The Cincinnati Review: "Black is the Color of my True Love's Hair"

The Normal School: "King and Lionheart"

Special thanks to Katy Masuga; Matthew Houck; Teddy Abrams, Lia Purpura, Danika Isdahl and, most importantly, my husband Jeffrey Skinner, who edited (with intelligence and great patience) the many versions of this collection.

In memory of Leslie Taylor McGrath

Books from Etruscan Press

Etruscan Press Is Proud of Support Received From

Wilkes University

Ohio Arts Council

Community of Literary Magazines and Presses

[clmp]

National Endowment for the Arts

Founded in 2001 with a generous grant from the Oristaglio Foundation, Etruscan Press is a nonprofit cooperative of poets and writers working to produce and promote books that nurture the dialogue among genres, achieve a distinctive voice, and reshape the literary and cultural histories of which we are a part.

Etruscan Press
www.etruscanpress.org
Etruscan Press books may be ordered from

Consortium Book Sales and Distribution
800.283.3572
www.cbsd.com

Etruscan Press is a 501(c)(3) nonprofit organization.
Contributions to Etruscan Press are tax deductible
as allowed under applicable law.

For more information, a prospectus,
or to order one of our titles,
contact us at books@etruscanpress.org.